MOTORCYCLE JOURNEYS THROUGH
THE ALPS AND CORSICA
SECOND EDITION

BY JOHN HERMANN

A Whirlaway Book
Whitehorse Press
North Conway, New Hampshire

A Whirlaway Book. Published by
    Whitehorse Press
    P.O. Box 60
    North Conway, New Hampshire 03860   U.S.A.
    Phone: 603-356-6556 or 800-531-1133
    Fax: 603-356-6590

Whirlaway and Whitehorse Press are trademarks of
Kennedy Associates.

ISBN 1-884313-12-4

5 4 3 2 1

Printed in the United States of America

WARNING!

Alpine roads and scenery and culture are known to
cause Alpinitis, a disease that creates an almost
uncontrollable urge to return. There is no cure. The
only relief is more Alpine riding, which results in
reinfection.

Dedication

All these roads have been discovered and enjoyed and played on and replayed on with such a wondrous company of friends as any person could hope for.

To ride the roads again, or to write of riding them, or to read of riding them, is to recall those good friends with whom they've been shared. Indelibly etched on my mind with each hairpin, each view, each culinary delight, is the memory of good friends who were there with me. To them, with the hope that they too remember, I would like to dedicate this book.

Until we ride again in the Alps.

▲ Contents

● ●

SOUTH OF ANDERMATT

EAST OF ANDERMATT

Karnten Land   **245**

C O R S I C A

A P P E N D I C E S

Motorcycle Journeys Through the Alps

NOTES:

o > Symbol indicates operating base
for one or more trips

> Only major autobahns and autostradas
are indicated on this map

> Trip numbers are in ovals 1-4

Near the top of the Furka Pass in Switzerland, the Finsteraarhorn dominates the western horizon. Under it, some of the best motorcycle riding in the world, the Grimsel Pass and the Furka Pass, meet down in the valley called Goms.

Here, several riders carve their way down Passo dello Stelvio in Italy. On Alpine roads there are no double yellows. You get no more road than you need or can claim.

▲▲ Foreword

● ●

My intention has been to make this new edition the best, and most complete, guide to the roads of the Alps available in any language.

Since the first edition came out in 1993, the good people at Whitehorse Press and lots of riding friends have indulged me as I explored further afield, turned up unpromising looking mountain roads, and also rechecked familiar roads and hotels. So here's a book chock full of new and updated stuff.

Clues about what to check out came from all kinds of places. Lots of maps. Hundreds of maps. Some show roads that other maps don't. Some show roads that aren't there. Some show roads that are foot trails. Some show foot trails that are roads. I've checked out each one. Once I offered a correction to a Swiss map company. They politely rejected my suggestion, and said that if they needed help on a map of California, they'd consult me. I had checked the Alpine road on the ground, and it is correct in this book if not on their map.

Once a friend at a Swiss hotel near Italy suggested an Italian Pass where all the maps showed nothing. Sure enough, it was there, and it is here.

In September of 1993, I was back exploring in the Alps when an American motorcyclist from New England showed me his copy of the first edition of this book—the first I'd seen. It was exciting to see it. Since then it's been fun to get to know, and get suggestions from, riders from all parts of the world. And from a few car drivers, too. One couple pointed out that there were two towns of the same name, and each had a castle, so when I said to turn at the town and go around the castle, there was a possibility of getting the wrong castle and the wrong road. So that's fixed here. European motorcyclists have shared their secret rides. I checked them, and if they worked, they're here.

My good friend Rob Beach and I have had fun trying to one-up each other: "Betcha' I found a road you don't know."

I'd been hesitant to endorse Yugoslavia, but he persuaded me to try the Slovenian national park. I did and it's here.

Since 1993, I've been back in the Alps a couple of months a year, probably, about another 40,000 miles.

And I've hounded book stores and shops all over Europe and America, buying lots of Alpine guide books, in Italian, German, and French, and even some in English. Many are aimed at motorcyclists. Some are pretty good. Many have beautiful pictures. But they often seem sort of parochial. The authors seem to have specialized on select parts of the Alps, or on certain kinds of roads, or perhaps just the most famous roads. Since the Alps are so full of roads, it is a challenge to be thorough and up to date. But that's what I believe is accomplished in this edition.

And Corsica. I'd heard about it. Now I've been there five times. You should try it. It's here in this book, too.

It's all been a lot of fun. I hope you find it so.

I've more experience riding than writing. But writing seems to be a good way to pass on some of the things I've learned. I hope this book will encourage you to explore and enjoy the Alps. Not only do I point you to the good roads, I hope to ease concern about things that might take trial and error and time and money to discover.

In writing, I find that I'm a bit uncomfortable using the first person: "I took this road," or "I recommend that souffle," or "I had the corner room with a view." My intention is that, except for this Foreword, I will seldom use the first person. The second person 'you' also bothers me, as it seems to separate me from you. Rather, I imagine that we're traveling together, or at least talking together, and I try to write as if we were discussing the roads and circumstances.

You should know that the maps don't always agree on the spelling of place names. Italian maps have their opinion, German maps insist on theirs, etc. Are Swiss maps a good compromise? I lean toward Swiss map maker Kummerly and Frey. They use readable color contrast and produce accurate maps of Switzerland and one of the Alps called Alpen Strassen (Alpine Routes). Recently Kummerly and Frey has marketed maps produced elsewhere, but packaged in their familiar blue folder. Some aren't so good. Fretag and Berndt

The endless supply of roads in the Alps includes lots of twisting and climbing. These hairpins on the east side of the Passo dello Stelvio in Italy regularly entertain riders.

has wonderful maps of Austria, and Touring Club Italiano has the best of Italy. Because none of the countries is square, most of the maps include detail of adjoining areas. I also use maps by Kompass, RV, Studio, F.M.B., Hallwag, and Michelin. I've tried verifying place names in the field, but road signs are often abbreviated, and sometimes I just forgot. To give you an example of the problem, I have two Austrian maps, printed in Austria. One says Solker Pass, one says Solk Pass. The Italian map calls it Solker. So do I. Some maps say Passo dello Stelvio, some say Passo di Stelvio.

In the high Alps, the road is THE road. There is no other. In lower elevations, roads proliferate, many going nowhere of particular interest. Consequently, some of the trips here in lower, more populated elevations have a bit more detail to help locate THE road that goes through and is worth exploring.

Here are some assumptions I've made while writing:

- German nouns are almost always capitalized. Italian and French nouns are capitalized, as in English, when they are the name of something. For example, Pass is always capitalized if it's German, but the French equivalent, col, and the Italian, passo, only when they're part of a name.

- I lean toward Anglicizing plurals of a few German and Italian words. The plural of the German word, Autobahn is Autobahnen. I say Autobahns. The plural of

Italian autostrada is autostrade. I say autostradas. Gelato, gelati, gelaterias. You get the idea. What I have written may not be completely correct linguistically, but I have tried to capture the international flavor while keeping the words familiar to other Americans.

- In the text, there will be no German umlauts or French accent marks. Their chief function is to guide pronunciation. There are some phonetic aids in the text.

- The French don't use the d' or l' in alphabetizing place names. In our index, Val L'Isere is under I, not L.

- St. is the abbreviation for Saint in French and Sankt in German. (It's Sankt Moritz.) Rather than make that distinction, I put both French and German saints alphabetically under "St." in the index.

I start the book at Andermatt, Switzerland, in the very middle of the Alps, a very good place to start a book or a trip. Then, in what I hope is an orderly and reasonable fashion, I describe every road and some facilities to the west, then to the south, and, finally, to the east of Andermatt.

You'll find most paved Alpine roads, and even a few unpaved ones, described here. Most have been tested many times in both directions, and all have been rated by stars—two stars (★ ★) shouldn't be missed! All are discussed as part of a trip that includes a home base, hotels, and attractions. The trips and bases can be combined to fit almost any time frame and interest.

We used the following conventions when making the maps:

MAP LEGEND

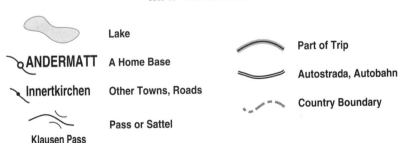

Lake	Part of Trip
ANDERMATT — A Home Base	Autostrada, Autobahn
Innertkirchen — Other Towns, Roads	Country Boundary
Klausen Pass — Pass or Sattel	

Worth a Special Trip

Imagine the most exciting, the most beautiful, the best possible motorcycle trip.

There'd be roads, endless roads, climbing and sweeping through forests, past waterfalls and glaciers, bursting out into meadows, twisting past snow-capped mountains.

There'd be green pastures with flowers and cowbells and farmhouses with flower boxes.

There'd be good food and shiny clean rest rooms, and maybe even motorcycle parking by the door.

And there'd be other motorcyclists, riding every kind of bike available on this planet.

Imagine this, and you've imagined the Alps. Motorcycle heaven with scenic overload.

There are other mountain ranges, but only in the Alps of Europe have people spent centuries building roads into each high valley and in between each peak. Only in the Alps can you expect good food and drink at the top of the mountain.

In the Alps, good roads, good food, good hotels, good health standards, and a standard of living to equal or exceed any other all come together with exotic scenery and a general appreciation of motorcycling and driving.

Starting on the Mediterranean coast, the Alps arc across Europe, cutting Italy's boot from the rest of the continent. Deep valleys cut the mountains from all directions. Since ancient times, people have been trying to get from one valley to the next. They hacked through gorges and hung roads on mountainsides, finally reaching a pass, into the next valley. The ancients must have agonized over which pass to risk, how to carry supplies for a long journey, how to trade with the natives. Now, those roads make a motorcycle paradise.

Just bring a credit card.

The south slopes of the Alps speak Italian, drink cappuccino, eat pasta at ristorantes and gelaterias, and drive Fiats and Moto Guzzis with skill on an amazing maze of mountain roads. They call a road over the mountain a *passo*.

The westerly slopes speak French, drink wine, eat French fries and glace and French bread at restaurants with French doors, and drive Citroens and Renaults (say "wren oh") over some of the highest roads in the Alps. They call a road over the mountain a *col*.

The north and east slopes of the Alps speak German, be they Austrian, Swiss, or Bavarian. They drink beer, eat Wienerschnitzel (cutlet Viennese style) and Eis (say "ice") at Gasthofs. They drive BMWs and Mercedes very seriously on spectacular roads. They call a road over the mountain a Pass.

There's something satisfying about a through road, one that goes up one side of the mountain and down the other side. In the Alps, such roads are known by the pass they traverse: Passo Sempione, or Grimsel Pass, or Col de l'Iseran. Each pass seems to have a unique personality.

At the Alps' core is Switzerland. We call it that. Germans living there call it *Die Schweiz,* the French call it *Suisse,* Italians who live there call it *Svizzera,* and Swiss stamps call it *Helvetia.* By any name, it's motorcycle heaven.

When the snow melts, Swiss put away their skis and get out their motorcycles. Motorcycling is so popular that German-speaking Swiss have a special slang for it: Toff (say "tough"). A Toffler, of course, is a biker. A Gasthaus may have a sign, *Tofftreffpunkt,* meaning a motorcycle meeting place. Tiny Switzerland even has its own motorcycle press, including a weekly magazine, *Moto Sport Schweiz,* published in both German and French, and a glossy monthly called *Toff.*

Most Americans will enter the Alps from international airports at Zurich, Munchen, Frankfurt, or Milano. Andermatt is almost as close to Milano's airport as Milano is.

Half a day and a ferry trip away is Corsica, the only close second to the Alps for riding. It's chock full of fun roads.

Imagine you and your bike in the high Alps at Andermatt, in *der Schweiz.* Every road in every direction is a great road. Select roads are marked here with a star. The *creme de la creme,* the absolute best roads, rate two. Some rate none, by Alpine standards, but those roads still must be among the best in the world. There isn't a bad one.

Coming down the west side of the Furka Pass, all of a sudden you're face to face with the Rhone Glacier. It's possible to park and walk into the glacier. It is the source of the Rhone River.

Alpine riders cross international borders often. Usually the border guard wants to see a passport only when it's buried deep under several layers of clothing.

Even though spring days are warm and long, last winter's snows are still deep in the high country, especially in hairpins. Here, on Nufenen Pass, a snow-blowing plow has opened the road.

Good Stuff to Know

Of Shower Curtains, Window Screens, Sealing Wax, and Hair Dryers

Okay, if the Alps are so great, how come:

1. There aren't any window screens?
2. Or wash cloths?
3. The shower curtains are too small or non-existent?
4. My hair dryer fries?
5. Double beds aren't?
6. The feather bed is too hot and too small?
7. The steak is tough?
8. Water's rationed?
9. There aren't any laundromats?
10. There's that extra appliance in the bathroom?
11. They can't count?

1. It's true. The Alps are full of cows and all. They tinkle their bells and so forth everywhere. And there are no window screens in the Alps. Mechanically, there isn't a double-hung window in the Alps. All windows are on hinges, so screens aren't handy, and so the finest establishment may have flies. Almost all hotel rooms have a sheer curtain that can serve as a screen at night.

2. In the Alps, only branches of American hotel chains have wash cloths. Others may have a tray of toiletries, needle and thread, a razor, and an assortment of towels of all sizes, but no wash cloths. If a wash cloth is important to your lifestyle, bring it from the New World.

3. For some reason, you're expected to sit down in the tub to shower with a hand-held shower on a flexible hose. So, why would you need a shower curtain? Some suggest that you are expected to wash before you shower. Maybe because Americans have flooded too many bathrooms, shower curtains are gaining a foothold in the Alps.

4.   American appliances will not fit European plugs, voltage, or cycles. European plugs are round, and the prongs are too. Adapters are available, but their use usually burns up the appliance and trips the circuit breaker, leaving everybody unshaven, undried, and in the dark. Some electric razors will switch to 220, and will work with an adapter. Some hotels have outlets in the bath good for 110 SHAVERS ONLY. They will not work with hair dryers. Hair dryers of modest price are available in Europe. Better to buy one there if it's absolutely needed. But they take up so much room! To save them and us the hassle, many hotels now have built-in hair dryers.

5.   Almost all double beds are two singles pushed together. Sometimes, expressing a desire for a *grand lit* (a big bed, say "grahn lee"), or a "matrimonial bed," will help.

6.   Everywhere that the Alps speak German—in Germany, Austria, north and west Switzerland, and the Sud Tirol part of Italy—beds have feather beds. A feather bed is like a giant pillow, or maybe a fat comforter. It rests in a big hump on the bed, which otherwise is more or less similar to a bed anywhere. That means there's a sheet on the mattress, but no blankets, no cover sheet, and no bedspread. Just a luxurious feather bed stuffed inside a washable cover. Feather beds vary in size and quilting. Without quilting, all the feathers may end up in one spot. Hardly ever will the thing cover the shoulders and feet at the same time. Some, in frustration, have been known to take the cover off the feather bed and crawl inside the cover. Better to curl up with the feather bed. It can be wonderful. If hot, leave a leg out, or more.

7.   Steak is not an Alpine specialty. The hills are alive with music . . . it's cow bells. *Cow* bells. Not bull bells or steer bells. Boy cows become veal. The Alps have wonderful veal in all kinds of creative ways. But steak is very likely a mature cow. Schnitzel is a cutlet, usually veal, but sometimes pork. Wiener Schnitzel can be either. Pork is usually cheaper.

8.   Drinking tap water is very American. It's not customary in Europe. There's absolutely nothing wrong with drinking tap water in the Alps. It is always safe. But Europeans don't think it's a nice thing to do in public. Most hotel operators know that Americans have the uncouth habit of

drinking water, even with meals, and they probably will make a modest carafe available upon request, but don't be surprised if the cook objects. It's reassuring to note that in the interest of safe driving, even the French have cut wine consumption dramatically in recent years, and Oktoberfest tents in Munchen are required to have alcohol-free drinks available. If it becomes an issue, get mineral water, with or without "gas." Some presumptuous hotels with stocked refrigerators in the room may have a little sign in the bathroom advising against drinking the tap water. It's a ruse.

9.   There are hardly any self-laundries in Europe. For whatever reason, entrepreneurs don't deem them worthy. Be prepared to hand-wash whatever needs washing. Detergent works better than soap. Finer hotels will have pricey laundry service.

10.   Hotel baths in Italy and France very often have bidets. They're for washing what's hard to wash in a basin. And for rinsing socks. (Don't be confused by the European use of the word "dusche." It means shower.)

11.   In Europe, the ground floor of a building is just that, the ground, the earth, terra firma. So the next floor up must be the first floor. And what Americans would call the third floor is clearly labeled "2," etc.

Rest Stops

A roadside Gasthaus, hotel, or restaurant is a logical rest stop in the Alps. It's diplomatic to order something from the bar before using the facilities. Coffee, tea, and hot chocolate come from the bar in Europe, and each is made one cup at a time. No refills. In the home of Swiss chocolate, hot chocolate is a cup of hot milk and a package of powder. (The real thing is in Italy.) A hot fudge sundae is always good in Switzerland and is called a Coupe Danemark. In Switzerland, Sinalco is a carbonated grapefruit drink, and Rivella tastes something like ginger ale. If you like the fizz, stop the waiter before the drink is dumped in a glass. There's always beer and wine, though most Euro restaurants feature only one local brew and few bars have hard liquor. Since the waiter will be charged for your order, pay and tip the waiter directly. In the Swiss countryside, the only currency is the Swiss Franc (a credit card slip signed in Swiss Francs will come home in dollars). If the bill is hand-written, remember that a European numeral "1" looks like an American "7," while Euro sevens have a horizontal line through them, and Europeans use a comma where Americans use a decimal point.

Spezi (say "SPAIT zee") is a cola drink available in Bavaria and Austria. Soft drinks are a little less varied in France and Italy, so mineral water may be a safe bet.

Cold drinks hardly ever have ice. Ice cubes (*Eiswurfel* in German) are a rarity.

When

When is the best time to ride the Alps? Spring? Summer? Fall? The best time is as soon as possible, of course.

Late spring, May, and June, are spectacular. Eighteen hours of daylight illuminate meadows carpeted with new yellow and blue flowers. Flower boxes have new geraniums. High mountains, still snow capped, are awesome backdrops to larch trees, just showing new green needles. Gorges are gorged with white water. Temperatures are moderate, yet the high passes cut through deep canyons of snow. Even the southernmost reaches of the Alps should be temperate. The only problem is that some passes may still be snowed in. Any pass needed for access or commerce will be open, but those just for playing on, the more remote ones, may be awaiting sun and snow plows.

Come summer, all the passes open, and the south warms up. Seldom are the Alps really hot by American standards, but Italy and the south of France can be. August is vacation time in Europe, so major areas can be peopled, and prices may reflect "high season." Flower boxes are masses of pink, red, purple, and yellow. Whole families rake and mow steep mountain meadows. Cow bells tinkle until dark.

Fall can turn the meadows pink. Mountain ash trees are loaded with orange berries. Near the tree line, larch needles are turning yellow. Last winter's deep snows are long gone and the mountains show rocky faces. Streams are drier. Days are shorter. Most of the tourists go home. Sometimes a passing weather front can dust the mountains with new snow, perfectly etching each formation and crevice. Fields of brilliant yellow-gold are "rape," a plant whose seed produces vegetable oil and biodegradable plastic.

Each Alpine country has special holidays. Sometimes, only one part of a country has a holiday. On one side of a pass, everything is closed. Across the pass, everything is open. Like in the U.S., holidays are arranged to make a three day weekend. Then everything closes and everybody goes someplace. In order to avoid arriving for a big trip only to find everything locked up, it's wise to check ahead. Many family run hotels and restaurants close for one day a week. In Germanic areas you may be greeted by locked doors and a little sign, "Ruhetag," quiet day.

Some claim that there is less rain in the fall but any season in the Alps is a good season.

What to Wear

Europeans *expect* motorcyclists to wear leathers. A motorcyclist in full leathers will be welcome anywhere in the Alps.

Ideally, wear full leathers as the primary article of attire with only underwear, and maybe a turtleneck, under them.

A rain suit should go on easily over the leathers. The simplest is a hip-length jacket over elastic-waisted pants. (The jacket goes on first, so you don't get soaked pulling on the pants and so either top or bottom can be entered easily for keys or passport or whatever, without removing the other part.) One-piece rain suits work fine at keeping water out, but they sometimes are hard to get into and out of, especially dancing on the edge of the traveled lane, or in a small WC (water closet; toilet—the term "rest room" is meaningless in Europe). Soleless, snap-on rain booties are effective and easy to use. Most rain boots are very hard to get on, and won't last if walked in. Remember, the boots go under the pants. Stores selling safety equipment have cheap and effective rain gloves to wear *over* leather gloves.

For cold, there should be a jacket to wear *over,* not under, the leathers. American softies have been known to enjoy an electric vest.

Leathers can be wiped off and debugged at the end of the day, and underwear washed in the basin if necessary, but jeans draped over the flower boxes on the balcony probably won't dry overnight.

Sport clothing, maybe just a colorful warmup suit, will last a long time between washings if it's worn only a couple of hours in the evening.

Two-Night Stands: A Home Base

When you're reading a tour brochure at home, it does seem exciting to actually contemplate 12 exotic hotels in two weeks. But that takes a lot of packing and unpacking and hotel adjustment to move lineally along the road. Instead, how about establishing a base camp in an interesting smaller town like Andermatt? That means at least a couple of days of baggage-free riding; convenient, almost familiar, stores and shops; and a familiar home base at the end of a great riding day.

Gas and Oil and Service and Tires

Some Alpine roads seem otherworldly, like a wild moonscape. But the Alps are not Siberia, or even Alaska. Even the most remote mountain pass is just a few kilometers from civilization. Europe has a well-motorcycled population. There are services and probably motorcyclists in every town and village, down at the bottom of the pass. And if you're at the top of the pass, everything is downhill.

Gas stations are plentiful, but not on mountain tops. Since they weren't in any medieval town plan, most are located outside the historical old parts of cities and towns and near the edge of smaller communities. Everything about a gas station looks familiar, with pumps and islands—everything, that is, but the price, which will be three or four times the U.S. price. Both gas and oil are sold by the liter. Leaded gas is being phased out, but both leaded and unleaded have higher octane than is available in the U.S.

In many smaller localities, stations close for a two-hour lunch at noon. Some stations announce that they are open (little signs, *aperto,* or *ouvert*), but only for drivers paying via automated credit card or cash machines.

Air is most likely available from a portable canister with a dial on the top. The canister hangs from a filler valve.

Usually, the dial has pressure readings in both metric and pounds. Take the canister over to your tire. It should have a plus and a minus button for pressure regulation. The metric unit of pressure is kilograms per square centimeter (usually called "bar"). One pound per square inch equals 0.07 bar; 33 pounds per square inch is about 2.33 bar. Finicky tire adjusters might want to carry a pocket gauge.

Most communities of any size have at least one motorcycle shop. At many the staff may appear busy even if they are not, so scheduling service in advance is wise. Store hours and days vary. Most depend on overnight delivery of parts from some central warehouse. Best way to find a shop is in the phone book, the yellow pages, or in motorcycle magazines, or by asking another biker. Smiles and pointing always help in an emergency. Pointing at a worn tire or a brake pad or a headlamp, etc., will register with most riders, dealers, and mechanics. They've probably been on the wrong side of a language barrier themselves.

An American on the Italian island of Sardinia once cracked a wheel hub on a BMW ST, not a very common bike. Calling around and using all possible translators, he learned about an overnight ferry from Sardinia to Genova on the mainland. The broken BMW was to take the ferry to Genova. Meantime, the BMW dealer in Genova would order a new hub from the BMW importer in Verona, Italy, and the hub would get to Genova overnight, too. The bike made it on the ferry. Other bikers on the ferry helped find the dealer in Genova. The hub arrived from Verona as scheduled, delivered by a 3-wheeled Lambretta truck. The wheel was laced and the American was off and running for the Alps that day.

Accelerating and braking and leaning on twisty roads all day long may wear tires faster than normal. Nothing spoils the enjoyment of a good road like worrying about a tire. Many motorcycle shops do not sell motorcycle tires. Tire stores do and usually they will mount them for you. A motorcycle dealer may send out to the tire store for the needed tire and then mount it for you. Dealers will want to follow the law, which requires them to mount only matching, factory approved tires.

Calling America

Most U.S. telephone companies have a "USA Direct" service. In each foreign country there's a toll-free number to call and the U.S. operator answers. It's cheaper and it's easier than dialing direct. The charge goes on your credit card or phone bill. Carry the numbers for the company you use. A call from a hotel room using the USA Direct number should not record on a hotel's billing machines.

	AT&T	MCI	Sprint
Austria	022 903-011	022 903-012	022 903-014
France	0800 99-0011	0800 99-0019	0800-99-0087
Germany	0130-0010	0130-0012	0130-0013
Italy	172-1011	172-1022	172-1877 (public phones may require coin)
Liechtenstein	0800 89-0011	0800 89-0222	155-9777
Switzerland	0800 89-0011	0800 89-0222	0800-89-9777

Calling Europe

It's really cheap during low-rate hours. Mid-day in Europe is early morning in the U.S.—the cheapest time to call.

In the U.S. dial 011 to get the international circuit. Then dial the country code (43 for Austria, 33 for France, 49 for Germany, 39 for Italy, or 41 for Liechtenstein and Switzerland), then the area code (for example, the area code for Andermatt is 41) and the desired number.

Most Europeans list their phone with the area code first, and a zero in front of the area code. The zero is like a "1" in America. Use it the same way. Dial it first to call out of the local area from within the same country. It isn't necessary if the call is originating inside that area, or if calling from another country. When calling to a European country from America or any other country, just use the country code and the area code. No zero.

Of course, the answering party may speak very fast in German or Italian or some other language. If uncertain, ask for "English, please."

Except for big city hotels, hotel staffs in Europe go to bed, so there may not be any answer in the middle of the night.

Almost every European business has a fax.

Demi-Pension

Almost every hotel in Europe will make a special price for "demi-pension," half pension, which is room, dinner, and breakfast. Full pension includes lunch. Quite often demi-pension is a good deal, and may be a necessity in remote locations. Sometimes there will be a choice available at dinner, sometimes not. Most of the time, breakfast is a buffet with a variety of wonderful fresh breads (no breakfast until the bakery has delivered), cold cuts, cheese, and possibly nowadays, juice and fruit, but hardly ever eggs.

Bread and rolls are delicious in Europe and are served at all meals. Most Europeans visiting the U.S. say what they miss most is good bread. Good beer is a distant second. In Europe, butter comes only at breakfast.

Demi-pension prices are per-person. Often a hotel is listed as a "garni," or "pension," usually meaning it has no public restaurant, although it should serve breakfast.

Cash Money

Border crossings are a regular fact of riding in the Alps. Alpine riders go back and forth across national borders often. On one side of the fence they may have good cappuccino, and on the other, not. But on either side it's advantageous, and possibly necessary, to pay in local currency. Credit card transactions are always in local currency, with the bank changing to dollars for billing. Austria is the only country where even waiters are prepared to deal in foreign currencies, although usually to their own advantage. So several purses or wallets are handy to keep each country's money readily available.

ATMs accepting American cards are available in many towns and villages. They spit out local currency. Back home you'll be charged in dollars.

Only major border crossings have currency exchanges. "Change" is often the identifying sign, although the German word is *Wechseln* and the Italian, *cambio*. Banks and train stations also usually have exchanges. In rural train stations, the ticket seller does the changing. Sometimes it's necessary to go to one teller to make the exchange, and then to a cashier to get the money.

In Europe, the custom is to wait in line to the right of the person being served. Waiting behind the person being served may lead the locals to assume that the ugly American is trying to crash the line (and vice versa). Watch what others are doing.

Some Italian crossings have auto club offices marked "ACI" (Auto Club Italia) that will change money. Hotels will change money, but often at a less desirable rate. All will charge a fee. Most of the time it's just as well to keep reserve funds in dollars. It's often cheaper to exchange traveler's checks than cash.

It's never advantageous to change twice, for example get Italian lira for dollars in Switzerland. There'll be a fee for changing to Swiss francs, then another for changing to lira (one lira, two lire).

How much things cost in terms of dollars depends on the exchange rate. When the dollar is strong, Americans feel European prices are a bargain and they buy things including motorcycles to take home. Sometimes the dollar is relatively weak and everything in Europe seems expensive and Americans only buy lunch and bring bikes from home. Then, when the dollar is strong and everything in Europe is a bargain, sometimes airfares aren't.

But whatever it costs, it's nice to have a little "real," that is local, money in your pocket.

Passports and Stuff

Border guards between countries in the European Union are fast disappearing. (Switzerland isn't in the Union.)

When there are guards (also at airports) there are two checks: a passport check, to identify the person; and a customs check to identify the "stuff." At most small border crossings in the Alps, the same official checks both. But there will still be two checks. The country you're leaving will check you out. Then, after you've crossed the border, the country you're entering will check you in. The two checks may be some kilometers apart. Usually, the customs folk are more interested in what natives may be bringing back than what visitors are carrying. With the coming of European union, there is less hassle, even about insurance, since it's assumed that everyone must be legal. Should a border guard note a non-European license plate, he'll very likely decide to check insurance papers. On some remote unstaffed crossings, a little sign may say something to the effect of, "If you have something to declare, stop in the next town."

Remember that you and your bike are passing through, not staying, so Americans don't need visas, but you must have a valid driver's licenses, and preferably an international one (available from auto clubs in the U.S.) as well as a passport.

A thin wallet on a string around your neck is handy for passports and official papers. Hiking, camping, and bicycle shops in America, and motorcycle shops in Europe sell inexpensive ones. A passport in your luggage is almost useless.

Photocopies of passport, driver's license, traveler's check numbers, vehicle registration, and airplane ticket (the big long ticket number is important should the ticket be lost) can be stashed in various bags.

So What Are We Going to Call It?

We call it Germany. Italians call it Germania. French call it Allemagne. But the Germans call it Deutschland.

We call it Lake Geneva. Germans call it Genfer See. The folks who live there call it Lac Leman.

We call it Venice. So do the French. The Germans call it Venedig. Italians call it Venezia. When you're there, Vienna is Wien, (say "vean.")

Most of us call it the Matterhorn. But half of it is in Italy where it's Monte Cervino. (And the Italian word for the German language is "tedesco!")

Most signs will be local. So will most maps. So, it's the intent here to use local names. The exception: herein it's Germany and Austria and Italy, not Deutschland and Oster-reich and Italia, even though that's what local signs will say (except in Italy, where signs pointing to Austria will say Austria). The international code is used everywhere in the Alps, and here: (D) is Deutschland, Germany. (A) is Oster-reich, Austria. (CH) is Die Schweiz, Switzerland. (I) is Italia, Italy. (F) is France. (FL) is Liechtenstein. Accordingly, Swiss bikes and cars are identified by a "CH" sticker, presumably for *Confederation Helvetia.*

Road signs usually emphasize pass names, along with some of the possible towns down the road, but not every possible town. Furka Oberalp is a railroad that carries vehicles. (Andermatt)

Germans put two dots over some vowels. They are called "umlauts" and are supposed to help in pronunciation. For example, there are supposed to be two dots over the u in Zürich and also over the u in München. Some texts leave out the dots but add an e, so it's Zuerich and Muenchen. That all seems confusing. Here, there will be no dots and no "e"s.

Sometimes Germans use a letter that looks something like a capital B (β) instead of a double "s" at the end of a word like "pass." Here, it will always be double "s".

And, Germans have the habit of tacking modifiers onto a word without spacing, so that a menu item might read "Grandmothersrecipeforsteakontoast," or a highway sign, "Oberalppass." Here it will be "grandmothers recipe for steak on toast," and "Oberalp Pass."

Besonder Uberwachung und Versicherung und Umleitung, or, "Special watching and insurance and detour"

Some German words don't slide easily from the English tongue. The French and Italian equivalents almost make good sense. But a couple of German words like those above are not in most handy "where is a good restaurant?" guides.

Besonder Uberwachung is on signs around Austria under a picture of a motorcycle. Motorcyclists will be especially watched! Other signs at Austrian borders advise that Austrian police use radar "in the whole land." Radar traps exist, especially in Austria. Typically, there is an unmarked radar in some area with a speed limit, like a village of a couple of houses, and the police wait farther along the road at the edge of the village and pull hapless drivers or riders over, waving them in with a red "ping pong" paddle. Friendly as Austrians are, their police will extract fines on the spot in cash for speeding. Most police in Europe do the same.

Police waved a bunch of motorcyclists into a big parking lot on the edge of Interlaken, in Switzerland. Seems there'd been a radar back in the town where the speed limit is automatically 50 kilometers per hour (about 30 m.p.h.) Each biker was fined on the spot, one modestly for a mere four kilometers over the speed limit, others several hundred Swiss francs. The police accepted Visa and Mastercard!

Recently, Austria has put signs along the road that show a motorcyclist with an angel above, and words to the effect of, "give your guardian angel a chance." Switzerland has had signs picturing a rider with the words "look out." Most auto drivers assume it is the rider who is supposed to look out! Both countries keep the motorcycles pictured up to date.

Helmets are mandatory in the Alps. Some countries require headlights at all times.

The international sign showing a motorcycle (usually ancient) in profile in a red circle means "motorcycles forbidden." The key is the little white sign underneath it, reading something like "between 2230 and 0600." There's often a second white sign that reads something like "except for bikes with business in the area."

Germany has a lot of low speed limit signs, even on Autobahns. The key is the little white sign underneath that says *Bei Nasse,* "when wet."

Versicherung, insurance, is mandatory. Proof of liability insurance is required before a vehicle license plate is issued in Europe. And it's expensive, like thousands of dollars a year. Many motorcyclists turn in their license plate for the winter to save money. Rental bikes should already be insured. Insurance should be included with any bike purchased in

Europe. Bikes brought from America must have proof of European insurance before they're allowed out of customs.

Americans living or stationed in Europe can get motorcycle insurance like car insurance. But few U.S. carriers will or can sell it to American motorcyclists traveling for pleasure. European insurance companies complain of bad luck with American bikers. Proof of insurance is a green piece of paper called a green card. That's what police and border agents will want to see. It should be in hand (or pocket) before operating on any European road.

European liability (and optional collision/comprehensive) insurance can be purchased for U.S.-registered bikes from these three sources:

Michael I. Mandell, Inc.; 410 Jericho Turnpike #202; Jericho, NY 11753-1318; phone: 800 245-8726; fax: 516 822-0172. Mandell can arrange shipping to and from Europe.

Warren Motorcycle Transport; phone: 800 245-8726; fax: 954 726-7336.

One of the German automobile clubs, A.D.A.C., has arranged convenient and reasonably priced liability-only green card insurance for touring Americans: A.D.A.C. Attention Mirjam Grundler; Jahnstrasse 26 D-88214; Ravensburg, Germany; phone: 49 751-23708; fax: 49 751-15352 (the 49 is the German country code, dial 011 49, etc. from the U.S.) She will need registration and drivers license numbers which can be faxed along with a credit card number. She'll mail you the green card. Request air mail.

Switzerland has a special organization for medical evacuation. It uses helicopters and jets to pick up sick or injured people and return them to Swiss hospitals. By special arrangements, it can operate from the roadside in nearby countries, flying directly to Switzerland. It is designed to serve Swiss nationals, but it also can serve members who pay a modest annual membership fee of about $20 (always listed in Swiss francs, but they accept checks in dollars). It communicates almost exclusively in German and its name is a twister, *Rettungsflugwacht,* which roughly translates to "emergency flight service." It's called REGA for short. It's designed to get Swiss nationals home from the Andes or Kansas as well as the Alps, a part of the service that Americans probably aren't interested in. Address: REGA, Mainaustrasse 21, CH-800B Zurich, Switzerland.

Fun mountain roads are labor-intensive, and the labor usually can only be done in summer, when the roads are open and the ice is gone. Detours are a possibility, labeled *deviazione* in Italian and *Umleitung* in German. Sometimes a portable traffic signal allows traffic past the repair area one way at a time. It's common, though not legal, for bikes to go to the front of any line waiting for the green, with the obligation, of course, to take off fast when the light turns green so as not to delay others. A tardy response to the green will elicit some angry responses from other drivers with whom the road may have to be shared. On popular bike roads, the light may collect quite an array of motorcycles, and the green light is almost like the start of a race. It does make sense to get ahead of any trucks or buses.

Where Are They From?

Everybody plays the game of guessing where their fellow travelers are from. License plates help. Cognoscenti can tell which town a long French license plate comes from. Some insist that shoes and socks (or lack thereof) are telltale. Chances are that any American will be identified as such without saying a word, especially while eating. Only right-handed Americans hold a fork in the right hand. Only Americans ever put the other hand below the table. Right-handed Europeans hold the knife in the right hand and the fork in the left. So, it's hard for an American to hide. In Europe, there have been plenty of wars, with bombings and occupations and refugees and invasions, unpleasant invasions of tourists as well as soldiers. Everybody has had plenty of opportunity to develop prejudices as well as preferences. In the long run, you might as well be identified as American as anything else.

Europeans all know of U.S. speed limits, and presume no American can go over 55. Keeping up with local traffic can be helpful as well as entertaining. British and Dutch drivers usually stand out because they have orange license plates. Both are usually very cautious in the mountains—the Dutch because they have no mountains to practice on, and the poor British because the driver is seated on the wrong side of the car and can't see the road ahead. At least both speak good English. (How far can you go speaking Dutch?) Locals are almost always more aggressive drivers than visitors.

A couple of American customs need modification in the Alps. The forefinger raised when ordering means two, like "two beers" (it is the second finger). The thumb raised means one beer. And the thumb and forefinger touching, the okay sign in America, is not okay in the Alps. The middle finger? Let's hope it's three beers.

News

In America, many newsstands carry *The European,* a British paper of continental news. It is a good way to find out what's happening in the Alps, including weather, road conditions, and status of Alpine passes. In Europe, most newsstands have three American newspapers, the *Herald Tribune, USA Today,* and the *Wall St. Journal*, all printed in Europe.

Road Signs and Drivers

Alpine signs almost always point toward towns and passes. Route numbers are obscure. It's best to know which town you're going to.

City limit signs are automatic speed limit signs, and villages and towns are where speed laws are usually enforced. Conversely, the end of a city, the city sign with a slash through it, means "resume highway speed."

Direction arrows often point *at* the road, which may not necessarily be the direction of travel. For instance, an arrow on the left side of the road pointing right most likely does not mean turn right. It means that "this is the road."

Schematic signs of anticipated intersections don't necessarily mean "now." There are often signs diagramming how roads will intersect in the next town.

You usually can't go around the block. If you miss a corner in a city, there probably will be another sign to the destination. If all else fails in a city or town, head back for the middle and start again. All towns have signs to the middle: *Stadtmitte,* in German, *centro,* in Italian. French have a wonderful sign: *toutes directions,* meaning "you can get anywhere going this way." The yellow diamond sign used in

Europe means "this road has the right of way over all entering or cross traffic." A slash mark through any sign means the end of it, whatever it was. A slash across a white circle means the end of whatever was being regulated, like the speed.

European drivers are usually very good and alert. Drivers' licenses are expensive and hard to get, and motorcycle licenses almost always require expensive schools and long periods of probation. European drivers will expect you to be competent and alert, too. If you are, they will usually accommodate you. Just remember, they consider the road to be a commodity in short supply. Anybody on it should be using it. Don't block the road. Some rules of the road and right of way are different than in America, and it sure helps to know them (for example, no turn on red in Europe, and no passing on the right on a freeway).

Skid marks on mountain roads are evidence that not all drivers have been perfect. Sometimes the marks head in unsatisfactory directions.

Each Alpine country has a tourist office in the U.S. Be warned, they are more into hiking than motorcycling.

Austrian National Tourist Office; Box 1142; New York, NY 10108-1142; phone: 212 944-6880; fax: 212 730-4568.

German National Tourist Office; 122 East 42nd Street, 52nd floor; New York, NY 10168-0072; phone: 212 661-7200; fax: 212 661-7174.

Italian Government Tourist Office; 630 Fifth Avenue, Suite 1565; New York, NY 10111; phone: 212 245-4961; fax: 212 586-9249.

Slovenian Tourist Office; 122 East 42nd Street, Suite 3006; phone: 212 682-5896; fax: 212 661-2469.

Switzerland Tourism; 608 Fifth Avenue; New York, NY 10020; phone: 212 757-5944; fax: 212 262-6116.

Time to ride.

Alps Pass Bagging List

How many of the 220 on this list can you bag?

To help you keep track of the passes you've bagged, here's a list based on their height in meters, in "descending" order, along with the country and trip in this book where you can find them. (Most are in the index, in alphabetical order along with all the other good places in the Alps.)

All the passes of the high Alps are on this list. That is, the ones that are roads. Some passes with names are little more than foot trails. They aren't on this list. A couple here have short unpaved sections, all noted in the text, but all can be enjoyed on road bikes. Highest is always best, just because it exists. The best rides are starred. Only pass roads that go over the mountain and down the other side are included. Dead ends don't count. Opinions as to elevations may vary. A meter here, a meter there, might change the rankings listed here. But the elevations seem to be from reliable sources.

The intention is to list every significant paved Alpine pass. There are a lot of passes at about 1000 meters or less that aren't significant. Major passes on Corsica are included in order of their height, but they're numbered separately. A pass road should cross a watershed. Some wonderful high Alpine roads go up a mountain and come back down into the same watershed, so they aren't on this list.

1. ★ ★2862 la Bonette (F) Trip 20
2. ★ ★2769 Col de l'Iseran (F) Trip 17
3. ★ ★2758 Passo dello Stelvio (I) Trip 29
4. ★ ★2744 Col Agnel (del Agnello) (F-I) Trip 19
5. ★2678 Col du Restefond (F) Trip 20
6. ★ ★2645 Col du Galibier (F) Trip 18
7. ★ ★2621 Passo di Gavia (I) Trip 30
8. ★2575 Grossglockner Hoch Tor (A) Trip 54
9. ★ ★2509 Timmels Joch (I-A) Trips 31 & 48
10. 2501 Umbrail Pass (I-CH) Trip 29
11. ★2478 Nufenen Pass (CH) Trip 2
12. ★2469 Col du Grand St. Bernard (CH-I) Trip 13
13. ★2431 Furka Pass (CH) Trips 1 & 2
14. ★2428 Grossglockner Fuscher Tor (A) Trip 54
15. ★2383 Fluela Pass (CH) Trip 28
16. ★ ★2361 Col d'Izoard (F) Trip 18
17. 2351 Col de Lombarde (I-F) Trips 19 & 20
18. ★2328 Bernina Pass (CH) Trip 29
19. ★2327 Col de la Cayolle (F) Trip 20
20. 2315 Forcola di Livigno (I) Trip 30
21. ★ ★2312 Albula Pass (CH) Trip 28

22. 2291 Passo di Foscagno (I) Trip 30
23. ★2284 Julier Pass (CH) Trip 27
24. ★2284 Col di Sampeyre (I) Trip 19
25. ★2244 Passo di Sella (I) Trip 39
26. ★2240 Col d'Allos (F) Trip 20
27. ★2239 Passo Pordoi (I) Trip 39
28. ★2233 Passo di Giau (I) Trip 40
29. ★2224 Susten Pass (CH) Trip 1
30. ★2214 Penser Joch (Passo di Pennes) (I) Trip 33
31. 2210 Passo d'Eira (I) Trip 30
32. ★2192 Passo di Valparola (I) Trip 39
33. ★2188 Col du Petit St. Bernard (I-F) Trip 13
34. ★2165 Grimsel Pass (CH) Trip 1
35. 2174 Col de Finestre (I) Trip 18
36. 2149 Ofen Pass (CH) Trip 29
37. ★2121 Passo di Gardena (Grodner Joch) (I) Trip 39
38. ★ ★2113 Splugen Pass (Spulga) (CH-I) Trip 27
39. 2111 Col de Vars (F) Trips 19 & 20
40. 2108 St. Gotthard (San Gottardo) (CH) Trips 2, 3 & 21
41. ★2105 Passo di Falzarego (I) Trip 39
42. ★2094 Jaufen Pass (Passo di Monte Giovo) (I) Trip 33
43. 2083 Col du Mt. Cenis (F-I) Trip 18
44. 2068 Col de la Croix de Fer (F) Trip 17
45. 2065 Passo del San Bernardino (CH) Trip 22
46. 2058 Col du Lautaret (F) Trip 18
47. 2057 Passo di Fedaia (Marmolada) (I) Trip 40
48. ★2052 Staller Sattel (I-A) Trips 44 & 53
49. ★2047 Passo Manghen (I) Trip 42
50. 2044 Oberalp Pass (CH) Trips 3 & 26
51. 2042 Eisen Tal Hohe (Nockalmstrasse) (A) Trip 58
52. ★2036 Bieler Hohe (Silvretta Strasse) (A) Trip 47
53. 2033 Sestriere (I) Trip 18
54. 2033 Passo di Valles (I) Trip 41
55. ★2017 Kuhtai (A) Trip 49
56. ★2006 Simplon Pass (Sempione) (CH) Trips 12 & 23
57. ★2002 Wurz Joch (Passo di Erbe) (I) Trip 42
58. 1996 Col de Larche (Maddelena) (I-F) Trip 19
59. ★1992 Passo di San Marco (I) Trip 37
60. ★1984 Col de la Madeleine (F) Trip 17
61. ★1971 Colle San Carlo (I) Trip 13

62. 1955 Passo di Rolle (I) Trip 41
63. 1951 Col du Glandon (F) Trip 17
64. 1948 Klausen Pass (CH) Trip 4
65. ★ ★1943 Passo di Croce Domini (I) Trip 37
66. ★ ★1922 Cormet de Roselend (F) Trip 13
67. 1920 Heiligenbach (Nockalmstrasse) (A) Trip 58
68. 1918 Passo di San Pellegrino (I) Trip 41
69. 1914 Lukmanier Pass (Lucomagno) (CH) Trip 3
70. ★1896 Passo di Mortirolo (I) Trip 30
71. ★1894 Hahntenn Joch (A) Trip 49
72. ★ ★1894 Passo di Tremalzo (I) Trip 36
73. 1883 Passo del Tonale (I) Trip 38
74. 1875 Passo di Campolongo (I) Trip 39
75. 1850 Col de Montgenevre (F-I) Trip 18
76. ★1828 Passo di Vivione (I) Trip 37
77. 1815 Maloja Pass (CH) Trip 27
78. 1805 Passo Tre Croce (I) Trip 43
79. 1805 Passo di Lavaze (I) Trip 42
80. 1793 Arlberg Pass (A) Trip 47
81. 1790 Sella Ciampigotto (I) Trip 44
82. 1788 Solker Tauern Pass (A) Trip 56
83. 1783 Turracher Hohe (A) Trip 58
84. ★1778 Col de la Croix (CH) Trip 10
85. 1773 Flexen Pass (A) Trip 47
86. 1773 Passo Forcella Staulanza (I) Trips 40 & 41
87. 1761 Furka Joch (A) Trip 47
88. 1760 Col de Joux Verte (F) Trip 15
89. 1760 Sella di Razza (I) Trip 44
90. 1759 Furkel Sattel (I) Trip 43
91. 1745 Passo di Costalunga (Karer) (I) Trip 42
92. 1739 Radstadter Tauern Pass (A) Trip 56
93. ★1712 Col du Joux Plane (F) Trip 15
94. ★1703 Col du Pre (F) Trip 13
95. 1700 Dr. Josef Mehrl Hutte (A) Trip 58
96. 1699 Cret de Chatillon (F) Trip 17
97. 1688 Passo Nigra (Niger Pass) (I) Trip 42
98. ★1685 Haiming Joch (Silzer Sattel) (A) Trip 49
99. 1682 Passo Campo Carlo Magno (I) Trip 38
100. 1679 Hochtannberg Pass (A) Trip 47
101. 1678 Col de Roubion (F) Trip 20

102. 1668 Col Valberg (F) Trip 20
103. 1668 Weinebene (A) Trip 59
104. 1656 Col du Lein (CH) Trip 13
105. 1644 Klippitztorl (A) Trip 59
106. ★1643 Glaubenberg Pass (CH) Trip 6
107. 1641 Katchberg Pass (A) Trip 58
108. ★1640 Col di Joux (I) Trip 14
109. 1636 Passo di Monte Croce (Kreuzberg) (I) Trip 43
110. 1633 Col des Saisies (F) Trip 13
111. 1631 Wolfgang Pass (CH) Trip 28
112. 1616 Passo di Brocon (I) Trip 41
113. 1613 Col de la Colombiere (F) Trip 15
114. ★1611 Glaubenbuelen Pass (CH) Trip 6
115. 1611 Vrsic Pass (SLO) Trip 60
116. 1608 Gurnigel Pass (CH) Trip 7
117. ★1601 Passo Duran (I) Trip 41
118. 1578 Col du Telegraphe (F) Trip 18
119. 1558 Piller Hohe (A) Trip 48
120. 1557 Nassfeld Pass (I-A) Trips 44, 53 & 60
121. ★1550 Pragel Pass (CH) Trip 4
122. 1547 Gaberl Sattel (A) Trip 57
123. 1547 Lenzerheide (CH) Trip 28
124. 1546 Col du Pillon (CH) Trip 10
125. 1542 Forcella di Lavardet (I) Trip 44
126. 1537 Monte Bondone (I) Trip 42
127. ★1536 Rossfeldringstrasse (D) Trip 51
128. 1531 Grand Colombier (F) Trip 16
129. 1530 Passo di Cibiana (I) Trips 40 & 41
130. 1526 Col de la Forclaz (CH) Trip 13
131. ★1526 Kartischer Sattel (A) Trip 53
132. 1518 Gampen Joch (I) Trips 33 & 35
133. 1509 Jaun Pass (CH) Trip 9
134. 1507 Gerlos Pass (A) Trip 52
135. 1504 Reschen Pass (Passo Resia) (A-I) Trips 32 & 48
136. 1502 Col du Chasseral (CH) Trip 11
137. 1500 Post Alm (A) Trip 55
138. 1491 Mattarone (I) Trip 25
139. 1487 Faschina Joch (A) Trip 47
140. 1486 Col des Aravis (F) Trip 15
141. 1486 Champex (CH) Trip 13

C-1. ★1477 Col de Vergio (F) Trip 61
142. 1476 Passo del Zovo (I) Trip 43
143. 1467 Col de la Croix Fry (F) Trip 15
144. 1461 Col des Montets (F) Trip 13
145. ★1458 Acherli Pass (CH) Trip 6
146. 1447 Col de Marchairuz (CH) Trip 11
147. 1445 Col des Mosses (CH) Trip 10
148. 1437 Panider Sattel (Passo di Pinei) (I) Trip 42
149. 1411 Col des Planches (CH) Trip 13
150. 1406 Ibergeregg (CH) Trip 4
151. 1400 Flattnitz (A) Trip 58
152. 1395 Passo Alpi di Neggia (CH) Trip 25
153. 1378 Passo di Cereda (I) Trip 41
154. 1374 Brenner Pass (A-I) Trip 48
155. 1369 Pas de Morgins (CH-I) Trip 15
156. 1363 Mendel Pass (Passo di Mendola) (I) Trip 33
157. 1362 Plocken Pass (I-A) Trips 44 & 53
158. 1360 Hebalpe (A) Trip 59
159. 1357 Dientener Sattel (A) Trip 54
160. 1336 Berwang (Namlos) (A) Trip 49
161. 1320 Col de la Faucille (F) Trip 16
C-2. 1311 Col de Sorba (F) Trip 66
162. 1294 Passo di Presolana (I) Trip 37
163. ★1293 Col de l'Aiguillon (CH) Trip 11
164. 1291 Filzen Sattel (A) Trip 54
C-3. 1289 Col de Verde (F) Trip 66
165. 1283 Vue des Alpes (CH) Trip 11
166. 1279 Weissenstein (CH) Trip 11
167. 1279 Saanenmoser (CH) Trip 9
168. 1278 Chrazeren Pass (CH) Trip 46
169. 1278 Rottenmanner Hohentauern (A) Trip 57
170. 1273 Pass Thurn (A) Trip 52
171. 1257 Col di Zambla (I)Trip 37
172. 1253 Aflenzer Seeberg (A) Trip 57
173. 1246 Seetaler Sattel (A) Trip 56
174. 1237 Col du Corbier (F) Trip 15
175. 1232 Prabichl Pass (A) Trip 57
176. 1229 Col de la Givrine (CH) Trip 16
177. 1227 Col du Mont Crosin (CH) Trip 11
C-4. ★1218 Col de Bavella (F) Trip 66

178. 1209 Fern Pass (A) Trip 49
179. 1204 Iselsberg (A) Trip 54
180. 1190 Sattelegg (CH) Trip 4
181. 1190 Passo Sella Nevea (I) Trip 60
182. 1180 Oberjoch (D-A) Trip 50
183. 1180 Col du Mollendruz (CH) Trip 11
184. 1176 Passo dell'Aprica (I) Trips 30 & 38
185. 1167 Schallenberg (CH) Trip 6
C-5. ★1163 Col de Vizzavona (F) Trip 65
186. 1163 Col des Gets (F) Trip 15
187. 1152 Col des Etroits (CH) Trip 11
188. 1150 Col de la Forclaz (F) Trip 17
189. 1150 Passo de Predil (I-SLO) Trip 60
190. 1135 Ramsau (A) Trip 56
191. 1126 Holzleitner Sattel (A) Trip 49
192. 1118 Ammer Sattel (A-D) Trip 49
193. 1110 Windische Hohe (A) Trip 60
194. 1097 Sudelfeld (D) Trip 51
C-6. 1094 Col de Sevi (F) Trip 63
195. 1093 Gaichtberg Pass (A) Trip 50
196. 1090 Wildhaus (CH) Trip 46
197. 1077 Kreuzberg Sattel (A) Trip 60
198. 1073 Wurzen Pass (A-SLO) Trip 60
199. 1060 Col de Richemond (F) Trip 16
200. 1056 Filzmoos (A) Trip 56
201. 1044 Balderschwang (D-A) Trip 50
202. 1015 Lahn Sattel (A) Trip 57
203. 1008 Brunig Pass (CH) Trip 6
204. 992 Potschen Hohe (A) Trip 57
205. 982 Gailberg Sattel (A) Trips 53 & 60
206. 969 Pass Gschutt (A) Trip 57
207. 963 Passo Zovello (I) Trip 44
208. 954 Pyhrn Pass (A) Trip 57
209. 941 Achen Pass (A-D) Trip 52
210. 940 Passo Durone (I) Trip 38
211. 903 Col de Tamie (F) Trip 17
212. 858 Kesselberg (D) Trip 51
213. 849 Ursprung Pass (D-A) Trip 51
214. 703 Passo di San Baldo (I) Trip 41

Around Andermatt

▲▲ Andermatt

Draw a straight line across the Alps from Milano, Italy, to Zurich, Switzerland. Right in the middle of that line, in the very middle of the Alps, is **Andermatt,** Switzerland.

Imagine you and your bike in Andermatt, in the mountain canton called Uri. There are four major Alpine trips over some of the highest passes through some of the most spectacular country in the Alps starting right in Andermatt. Uncluttered by cities, these trips are good in any order, in any direction.

The village of Andermatt, at 1450 meters, is almost as high as Zermatt. Zermatt has the Matterhorn and hoards of tourists. But Zermatt doesn't have any roads. Andermatt does.

For centuries, Andermatt was the crossroads of the Alps: Italy to the south, France to the west, Germany to the north, Austria to the east. Now, thanks to the longest highway tunnel in the world, tour buses and trucks, everybody with fear of heights, and anyone with urgent business, all go through the mountain instead of through Andermatt. Andermatt is for Alpinists and motorcyclists. That's what this book is about—

Andermatt has gas stations, restaurants, hotels, and shops along a cobblestone street with granite slabs. Most everything about the gas station will seem familiar—except the price.

where the crowds don't go but motorcycles do.

Park by the cafe of the Hotel Monopol-Metropol in Andermatt. You're on the inside corner of one of the best sweeper roads in the world, the **Oberalp Pass.** It starts right there at the hotel. The first sweep goes around the hotel. The road continues, arc after arc of smooth asphalt, never straightening out, up the face of the mountain.

In mid-summer, it's light until after 10 p.m., and bikes come from the great cities in the valleys to drive the Oberalp in the evening. The pass is worth several passes. (Mind the decreasing radius in the tunnel, coming down.)

Looking down from the sweepers of the Oberalp, you can see Andermatt huddled in a corner of its mountain-ringed valley, some modern buildings, some shingled chalets, some log buildings, with a Baroque church tower above all. The cobblestone main street has smooth granite slabs for wagon wheels. The street looks ancient, but was brand new in the 1980s.

A hypotenuse bypass leads across the valley from the granite Kaserne (military base) toward the **St. Gotthard Pass.** A cable car goes from the west side of the village up on Gemsstock Mountain, 1500 meters above the town. The cog railway weaving around the Oberalp road leads down to a train station in Andermatt, where it meets two other cog lines. This is the land of the Glacier Express train between Zermatt and St. Moritz.

Andermatt has restaurants, gas stations, banks, shops, and

From the Hotel Monopol-Metropol, watch the parade. From all over the world, riders come to the sweepers of the Oberalp Pass. The first sweep goes right around the hotel.

the Post, Switzerland's post office, telephone exchange, and bus station. You can dial anywhere in the world from the Post and pay when the call is completed. Just remember that the east coast is six hours behind the Alps, and the west coast nine hours. So 6 p.m. in Andermatt is noon in New York and 9 a.m. in California. All the Alps have daylight savings time. They just start and end on different dates than ours in the U.S. and even than other countries in Europe.

The Post is where all those yellow buses park, the public buses that deliberately motor into every cranny of Switzerland, sometimes towing a baggage trailer and tootling their three-note horn. The horn is supposed to send all other traffic scrambling to get out of the way. Most importantly, the Post sells freeway stickers, called "vignettes," that all vehicles must have to drive on a Swiss freeway, including many tunnels and many two-lane roads that have limited access. Swiss vignettes are annual. The vignette does not substitute for tolls, and there are a couple of toll roads in Switzerland. (Austria also requires a vignette to use the Autobahn, although Austria has short term ones, good for a week or a month).

Andermatt's travel bureau is: **Verkehrsburo;** CH-6490 Andermatt, Switzerland. (In Euro addresses the ZIP comes before the town. In this instance, 6490 is the ZIP, CH is the code for Switzerland.) Phone: 041 887-1454; fax: 041 887-1185.

A sampling of the many hotels in Andermatt includes:

Keep the bike on that granite slab! On the crook of the cobblestone street through Andermatt, right where the street crosses over a mountain stream, is the Hotel Drei Konige. Behind are sweepers of the Oberalp Pass.

The **Hotel Monopol-Metropol,** on the corner where the Oberalp begins, is a building with an international flavor and a kitchen that blends Swiss and French cooking. CH-6490 Andermatt; phone: 041 887-1575; fax: 041 887-1923.

The **Drei Konige Hotel** (three kings, as in "We Three Kings of Orient Are") is located in the crook of the cobblestone street through Andermatt, right beside a rushing mountain torrent. It's traditional Swiss. CH-6490 Andermatt; phone: 041 887-0001; fax: 041 887-1666. The German author, Goethe, stayed at the Drei Konige in the 18th Century. It's been updated since.

The **Sporthotel Sonne** (sun) is a multi-story log building in the village center, with a door that opens directly onto the cobblestone street. It's much more modern than it looks, with a cozy dining room and a garage for motorcycles. CH-6490 Andermatt; phone: 041 887-1226; fax: 041 887-0626.

In Switzerland, those proposing to build a new building must erect a scaffolding to show the actual size and shape proposed. Then those concerned can see what view might be affected, and what shadow cast. Such was the case for the Alpenhotel Schlussel in Andermatt. The scaffolding was up for years. But now, there's a brand new hotel. **Alpenhotel Schlussel;** CH-6490 Andermatt; phone: 041 888-7088; fax: 041 888-7089.

In any language, Swiss money is called a Franc. Traveler's

Bikes charge a hairpin on the Furka Pass that's been modernized by extending it on stilts over space. That's more of the Furka continuing on the left down to the village of Gletsch. The Grimsel climbs the far slope.

checks and money can be changed at a bank or at any Swiss train station.

German is the working language of Andermatt, but most locals can speak some English. The waitress may be a Norwegian who spent her last holiday in San Francisco, while the clerk in the sport shop very likely can discuss slopes at Aspen.

Besides the Oberalp Pass heading east, three roads lead out of Andermatt. West across the valley beyond Andermatt, the **Furka Pass** snakes up the mountain. Compared to the Oberalp, it's narrow and tight and irregular. Working up the mountain south is the St. Gotthard Pass. To the north an unbelievable road squeezes down through a gorge called the Schollenen, made by the Reuss River.

Information on road conditions in English can be obtained from Swiss auto clubs: ACS (Automobilclub Schweiz); Bern, 031 312-1515; TCS (Touring Club Swisse); Geneve; 022 735-8000.

The road snaking up the west side of the Susten Pass cuts through the mountain, while a mountain stream goes over it, and then becomes a waterfall.

Trip 1   Furka, Grimsel, Susten

• •

Distance   *About 120 kilometers from Andermatt*

Terrain   *Steep twisting climbs into glacier worlds, three steep twisting descents, plus the narrow Schollenen gorge, mostly modern highway. Some tunnels*

Highlights   *Rhone Glacier, Aareschlucht water storm, favorite motorcycle cafes, Sherlock Holmes site, Devil's Bridge and stone, Autobahn tunnel entrance, ★Furka Pass (2431 meters), ★Grimsel Pass (2165 meters), and ★Susten Pass (2224 meters), the Schollenen Gorge, Oberaare road*

At 2431 meters, the Furka Pass is one of the higher roads in the Alps. Just a few kilometers from Andermatt, up among glacial peaks and rushing water, it's easy to feel civilization is very far away.

West from Andermatt the road follows the Furka-Oberalp cog train, the route of the Glacier Express, through Hospen Tal, a village with a stone watch tower, and where the St. Gotthard Pass road turns up and south. The cog train and the Furka road continue on west across the valley to Realp where the train enters a tunnel under the pass. (So the Glacier Express folk never see the pass or its glaciers. They ride the train through the tunnel in the dark. When the pass is closed, cars and bikes have to take the train, too.)

Across the top, on the west side, there's a parking lot on the south side of the road. From it there's a magnificent view of the Rhone Valley, called the **Goms,** and the mass of the Rhone Glacier, and the cantilevered hairpins of the Furka road down below, and the zig zags of the **Grimsel Pass** road climbing the far mountain, and the lake at the top of the Grimsel, and the peaks beyond, and . . .

Climb down below the edge of the parking lot. Look closely. The lot is atop a gun emplacement that commands the whole scene. It's so well camouflaged that it defies detection just a few feet away.

The westerly side of the Furka is mostly new alignment. Then at one hairpin, you're face to face with the **Rhone Glacier.** Drive right up to the base of the ice, source of the Rhone River. Water melting from this glacier runs to the Mediterranean at Marseille, France. (Back at Andermatt, all the water was running to the Rhine and the North Sea.) At the glacier there's a parking lot terraced on the edge of the mountain, with an outdoor cafe that's popular with bikers. Restrooms are down under the parking lot. A tunnel carved into the glacier permits a walk into the blue world inside.

It's only 31 kilometers from Andermatt, across the Furka Pass and past the Rhone Glacier, down to **Gletsch,** where the Grimsel Pass road intersects and heads up and north. Gletsch

After a fun-filled ride up the hairpins and twisties of the Susten Pass, most bikers are ready to kick tires a minute and perhaps check the scene from the terrace of the restaurant. Bikes often pack the parking lot.

is just a couple of stone buildings at the tree line.

Once some American bikers got trapped at Gletsch by avalanches and mud slides on the pass roads. The Grimsel was closed. The Furka was closed. The Goms road west was closed. The stone hotel building had no electricity. But the cog train was running back and forth through the Furka train tunnel. So, the bikers went down below Gletsch to **Oberwald** and put their bikes on a flat car. They sat on the bikes through 25 minutes of dark tunnel and debarked at **Realp** over by Andermatt.

The traversing road up the Grimsel from Gletsch leads to hairpins supported by walls of massive stones and offering great views of the Rhone Glacier.

Several restaurants around the lake at the top of the Grimsel (don't ask the lake's name) are popular with motorcyclists. The one farthest north, Hotel Alpenrosli, has a large parking area marked for motorcycles only. It's often full of bikes, while the riders enjoy the sunny restaurant terrace.

Just west of the Hotel Alpenrosli (to the left, facing the hotel) is a tiny short road you have to try if it's open—the **Oberaare.** It looks like a driveway with a traffic light. About ten kilometers long, it snakes up high above the top of the Grimsel Pass and then down to a lake, the Oberaare See. Views are awesome . . . glaciers, snow-capped peaks, icy white lakes, and the ribbon of the Grimsel Pass road winding down north. Traffic is one way at a time, controlled by the traffic light at each end of the road.

It's only 37 kilometers north from Gletsch, across the Grimsel, past the Hotel Alpenrosli, down past dams and lakes and hydroelectric plants and through several tunnels, one of which has a decreasing radius curve, into forests and through meadows to **Innertkirchen,** where the **Susten Pass** road heads east. This is countryside known in song and story as the Berner (Bernese) Oberland, canton Bern, the valley of the Aare River. Just a few kilometers below Innertkirchen, the Aare goes through a very narrow gorge called a *Schlucht,* as in *Aareschlucht.* It's a spectacular display of enormous volumes of frothing water. There's a parking lot on a hairpin where a wooden catwalk leads into the water storm.

Just below the Schlucht is the base of the **Reichenbach Waterfall,** the great cascade where Arthur Conan Doyle had Sherlock Holmes fall to his death in a fight with the villain Moriarty. A marker at the base of the falls says it happened on May 4, 1891. It must be so, because the monument was erected by "The Norwegian Explorers of Minnesota!" There's a statue of the great detective in the nearby village of **Meiringen.** (Meiringen and the roads of the Berner Oberland are in the next chapter, Trips 5, 6, 7, and 8.)

The climb up the Susten Pass from Innertkirchen goes from meadows back up to the land of glaciers. The parking lot at the top of the Susten Pass, surrounded by glaciers, is another favorite motorcycle gathering place. The restaurant has a view terrace from which there's free access to the restrooms below (Euro restrooms are usually marked "WC").

The road east is a tunnel. Sit on the terrace and try to identify the bikes coming from the east by their exhaust note magnified in the tunnel. Some of the road beyond the tunnel was taken out by an avalanche, and the temporary replacement was one-lane, one-way-at-a-time in accordance with posted times. You were on your honor, using your own watch or clock. Often, bikes gathered in significant numbers to start down at the appointed time.

It's 53 kilometers across the Susten Pass from Innertkirchen on the west to **Wassen** on the east. The final curves down into Wassen offer views of one of the major engineering feats of the Alps, the four-lane freeway in the gorge of the Reuss River. It connects Zurich with Italy through the St. Gotthard tunnel. The gorge is so narrow and steep that the road is either on a bridge or in a tunnel. Here it's called an Autobahn, and it leads to the tunnel under Andermatt, the longest vehicle tunnel in the world. The tunnel daylights as an autostrada in **Airolo.** (See Trip 2).

It's only a couple of kilometers south, up the Schollenen gorge from Wassen to Goschenen, where the freeway enters the long tunnel, and where the really steep part of the gorge begins. The main line of the railroad goes in a tunnel, too, leaving only a cog line to grind on up to Andermatt alongside the hairpins of the gorge road. (There's a fun dead-end road westerly from Goschenen to a high Alpine dam and lake called Goscheneralp.)

By the freeway entrance to the long tunnel is a giant rock with the flag of canton Uri on it: gold, with a black bull's head with a ring in its nose and a red tongue hanging out. The big rock was moved aside at great expense during freeway construction because:

> Long ago, the villagers failed to get a bridge across the gorge. The devil offered to build it in exchange for the soul of the first to cross the bridge. But the villagers fooled the devil by sending a goat across the bridge first. Enraged, the devil hoisted the huge rock to smash the bridge, only to drop the rock when a villager made the sign of the cross.

The rock's still there to prove it. Pictures of the **Teufelbrucke (Devil's Bridge)** abound around Andermatt.

The climb up the gorge toward Andermatt goes right by the Devil's Bridge and another bridge of Roman origin. And there's a spot in the gorge that will be forever Russian. A turn-off near the Devil's Bridge leads down to an enormous carving in the mountainside with script in Cyrillic. Seems it commemorates a Russian army. Defeated by Napoleon on the plains, it retreated south and was trapped in the gorge.

A monument out in front of the museum atop the St. Gotthard Pass commemorates early attempts to fly over the pass. The museum traces valiant efforts to conquer the pass, culminating in the present road of sweeping curves.

The monument's named after the Russian general, Suworow. Turn into the monument parking lot and continue on down the old gravel road over the old Teufelbrucke. (The road is closed to cars.) The best view of the monument is from this road. (For other Russian monuments in the Alps, see Trip 56, Filzmoos and Tauern Passes, and Trip 60, Three Country Loop.)

A final short tunnel opens out onto the high Andermatt valley. The main road is the hypotenuse bearing right toward the St. Gotthard and Furka Passes. A mini interchange leads into the village, past the vast stone Kaserne, home to much of Switzerland's citizen army. In the village, soldiers patrol around and occasionally roar by in rubber-treaded tanks, or astride an army Condor motorcycle, assembled in Switzerland with a Ducati engine.

Remember the DB-1 Bimota that was on the cover of every bike magazine once? There it was, parked in Andermatt. Tiny, beautiful. Tracked down, the owner allowed as how it had indeed cost a bundle of Swiss Francs. "You could have bought a Harley for that!" The owner reached into a pocket and pulled out a card. He was a Harley dealer.

On long summer evenings, bikers come from the great cities of Europe, not to mention the rest of the world, just to ride the sweepers of the Oberalp Pass above Andermatt.

Trip 2 St. Gotthard, Nufenen, Furka

Distance	*About 110 kilometers from Andermatt*
Terrain	*Three steep twisting climbs and descents, mostly modern highways*
Highlights	*St. Gotthard Museum, a favorite motorcycle cafe, concrete-roofed sweepers, in and out of Italian-speaking, cappuccino land, St. Gotthard Pass (2108 meters), ★Nufenen Pass (2478 meters), ★Furka Pass (2431 meters)*

It's a good sweeping ride up the St. Gotthard to the top, where all of a sudden, it's no longer the St. Gotthard, but the San Gottardo. The south slopes of the Alps speak Italian, eat pasta, and drink cappuccino, even in Switzerland. The old-time hospice at the pass summit has been turned into a museum of the historic attempts to conquer the pass, including the history of the Devil's Bridge. Water here runs to the Po River in Italy, and thence to the Adriatic. A monument out front commemorates aviators' attempts to conquer the pass. Crossing the Alps in early planes was a major undertaking.

Behind the museum there's a short stretch of the old cobblestone road down to the south. It's very photogenic but not a lot of fun to ride. It's usually closed to through traffic.

A lot of the southern slope of the San Gottardo is in kilometer-long, covered concrete sheds, to protect motorists from avalanche. The sheds are open on one side, and the road surface is good at highway speed.

The longest vehicle tunnel in the world, the one that enters the mountain as an Autobahn at Goschenen on the north side of Andermatt, comes out on the south slopes of the pass at Airolo as an autostrada, having passed under all these good roads. By following the signs for **Passo della Novena** (that's what the Nufenen is called in Italian) it's possible to avoid getting involved in the tunnel traffic at Airolo. The Nufenen, a newly laid out road and one of the highest in Switzerland, climbs west out of Airolo.

Often photographed are the **three flags** flying at the top of the Nufenen, the Swiss flag flanked by those of the two cantons connected by the pass, Ticino and Wallis. Behind the flags, way across the Goms valley, are the peaks of the Berner Oberland, including the Jungfrau. The most prominent as viewed from the Nufenen is the Finsteraarhorn at 4274 meters.

The cafeteria at the top of the pass is popular with bikers, because the northerly descent, way down into the Goms at **Ulrichen,** is a wonderful piece of road: good pavement, steep, and full of predictable hairpins.

Ulrichen is down in meadowlands, so it's a real climb back up and east to Gletsch where the Furka and Grimsel meet. The road passes some military airstrips and the railroad loading ramps at Oberwald, where cars and motorcycles can be driven right onto the train for a tunnel ride under the Furka Pass back to Andermatt. Should you choose this method, just ride onto a flat car and take a seat in a passenger compartment, or maybe sit on your bike. Switzerland claims to be planning a steam cog train using the old abandoned tracks over the pass.

Climbing up to Gletsch from Oberwald the awesome switchbacks of the Grimsel Pass are straight overhead. They've been rebuilt in recent years. There's lots of concrete behind those huge stones.

The parking lot of the Rhone Glacier revealed a bunch of bikes, including a YB-1 Bimota. The rider turned out to be a dentist from Disentis, over the Oberalp from Andermatt. "Your English sure is good." "Oh, I teach part time at the University of Illinois!"

Trip 3   Oberalp, Lukmanier, St. Gotthard

Distance	*About 154 kilometers*
Terrain	*Three climbs and descents, plus a valley run*
Highlights	*Oberalp Pass (2044 meters) and the world's best sweepers, less-traveled Lukmanier Pass (1914 meters), St. Gotthard Pass (2108 meters), a taste of Romansch culture, deeper into Italian-speaking Switzerland*

Sweep up the Oberalp from Andermatt into canton Graubunden (sometimes called Grisons in English), where buildings are usually stucco with arches and deep set windows and stenciled decoration. The official language is Romansch. Nobody speaks it, but they print signs in it. The working language remains German. (Elementary school children in many parts of Graubunden are taught in Romansch.)

Across the Oberalp, at a pretty good sized town called **Disentis-Muster,** the **Lukmanier Pass** road heads south. Disentis is famous for a big monastery church visible just above the town. To visit it, you have to park below on the main road and hike up. The interior is sort of Spanish baroque. To head for the Lukmanier, take a sharp right in the middle of the town down across the Vorderrhein River. The sign for the pass in Romansch will be *Cuolm Lucmagn.* As soon as you cross the pass, the signs will be in Italian, and the pass will be called Passo del Lucomagno. The pass road is modern all the way to Biasca. There's a functional restaurant at the top of the pass.

A pleasant stop might be the **Hotel Olivone and Post,** CH-6718 Olivone, about eighteen kilometers down the Ticino (south) side. Phone: 091 872-1366; fax: 091 872-1687.

The Passo del Lucomagno meets the San Gottardo autostrada at a town called **Biasca.**

Biasca is in one of those major valleys that cut deep into the Alps, the **Valle Leventina.** It's the best route from the great cities of Italy to Zurich, via the long St. Gotthard tunnel. So a lot of traffic is heading for the St. Gotthard (called *San Gottardo* here), and since it's about 35 kilometers north, the autostrada may be the viable route to get there. Just be sure to exit the autostrada at Airolo, or you'll be treated to at least 20 minutes of tunnel behind a diesel-belching bus or truck, all the way to Goschenen.

On the climb up the St. Gotthard from Airolo there are a couple of tight sweepers on stilts out over the valley, with big metal expansion joints that are slippery when wet. A turnout has a little restaurant with a fine view of the can-of-worms interchange squeezed into the valley down in Airolo where the autostrada, the tunnel, the Nufenen Pass and the St. Gotthard Pass roads all meet.

A Kawasaki pulled into the restaurant at the top of the Lukmanier once. The rider was all in white—white leathers, white boots, white gloves. He allowed he worked for Swissair. "How do you keep it white?" "Oh, that's my wife's job!"

Trip 4   Klausen, Pragel, the 'eggs'

Distance   *About 200 kilometers from Andermatt*

Terrain   *Tight climbs and descents on narrow, less-traveled roads*

Highlights   *William Tell country, a historic highway on lakeshore, Klausen Pass (1948 meters), Switzerland's little-known ★Pragel Pass (1550 meters), Ibergeregg (1406 meters), Sattelegg (1190 meters)*

Dash north down the Schollenen Gorge from Andermatt and hop on that Alpine masterpiece, the Autobahn, down toward **Luzern.** In a couple of minutes, you'll be in **Altdorf,** almost at sea level, at least the level of **Lake Luzern. Klausen Pass** climbs east from Altdorf.

Altdorf is famous as the home of William Tell and there's a monument and statue of him and his son in the center of the town. Tell was not just a good marksman, but a symbol of Swiss independence. The guy who had him shoot the apple off his son's head back in the middle ages was the evil count, an outsider. It seems that four of the Swiss forest cantons around Lake Luzern decided they'd like to be independent. The count was against it. Tell was for it. The evil count dreamed up the ultimate punishment for a father—the life of his son. He was sure that the son would flinch or Tell would miss, or bóth. We all know that the son didn't and Tell didn't.

The lake that we call Lake Luzern the Swiss call by the tongue twister Vierwaldstatter See (four forest state sea) after the four cantons of Tell's day. And we call the country "Switzerland" after **Schwyz,** one of the four forest cantons.

There's a helpful and well stocked Kawasaki-Yamaha

On the inside of a 180 on the Klausen Pass is the attractive Hotel Posthaus Urigen. It advertises itself as a motorcycle meeting place.

shop called Gisler Motos at Shattdorf, on the main road just south of Altdorf.

Climbing out of Altdorf on the Klausen, the next village is **Burglen,** Tell's home, where there's a smaller statue of Tell.

About halfway up the Klausen from Altdorf, on the inside of a 180, there's an attractive hotel and restaurant called **Hotel Posthaus Urigen.** It's handsomely decorated inside and out and advertises itself as a motorcycle meeting place. (Hotel Posthaus Urigen; CH-6465 Urigen; phone: 041 879-1153.)

East of the Klausen summit, still in canton Uri, the road crosses a high, mountain-ringed valley called Urnerboden. It's open range populated by cows. Thousands of cows. Signs beg vehicles to stay off the pastures. It's also desirable to dodge cows and cow pies.

Near the bottom, on the northeast side of the Klausen in canton **Glarus,** are some narrow one-way cobblestoned tunnels. Traffic is controlled by a traffic light at each end.

Down below the Klausen in the town of Glarus, the road to the **Pragel Pass** intersects, but the pass is so small and remote that there's no sign for it. Watch for a sign pointing to the left, west, to Klon Tal or Klon Taler See (*Tal* added to a German word means valley).

The road is two lanes as far as the lake, Klon Taler See, where there's a modern terrace restaurant and hotel called Rhodannenberg (**Hotel Rhodannenberg;** CH-8750 Klon Tal; phone: 055 640-7161). The rest of the road over the pass is one paved lane and has a feel like maybe nobody's ever been there. But a long period with no oncoming traffic doesn't mean there isn't a logging truck around the next corner. The asphalt is smooth but has a significant lip on each edge. It follows the lake for several kilometers, where there are triangular warning signs advising drivers to look out for frogs. Across the lake are sheer vertical cliffs of almost a thousand meters. Spectacular. Looks like Lake Louise at Banff in Canada.

Signs along the road with lengthy passages in German say that this part of the road is not open to traffic on weekends. The same signs greet the rider coming from the other direction across the pass at Muota Tal, the valley on the other side. Muota Tal leads down to Schwyz, the town the country's named after. (Heading for the Pragel from Schwyz, follow the signs to Muota Tal, as there are none for the pass.)

At Ibach, next to Schwyz, the main road passes the Victorinox factory, one of the "original Swiss Army Knife" factories. Showrooms have everything for sale. Down a little lane near the factory is a BMW dealer. From Schwyz, the main road back toward Altdorf and Andermatt is called the **Axenstrasse** because it was carved by ax from the steep cliffs around Lake Luzern, Vierwaldstatter See.

Until recently, the Axenstrasse, hanging on the east side of the Vierwaldstatter See, was the only way around the lake toward the St. Gotthard. Now, there's a four-lane Autobahn tunnel through the cliffs on the other side of the lake, where before there was no road of any kind. (Following the lake in the opposite direction, actually west, from Schwyz, there's a ferry across the lake to **Beckenried** and connections with the roads of the Berner Oberland, Trip 6. There's a good hotel at the ferry landing across the lake.)

A lesser pass, the **Ibergeregg,** 1406 meters and heading northeasterly, starts in the middle of Schwyz, by the church. The view over Vierwaldstatter See from the restaurant at the top is great. Little-trafficked and heavily forested, the Ibergeregg comes down by a couple of lakes and a huge pilgrimage church at Einsiedeln, not far from Zurich. The church is of modest historic or artistic interest, but it is big.

Short of Einsiedeln, a one-lane road (with a few meters unpaved) crosses a handsome covered bridge and snakes over a woodsy ridge called **Etzel** coming down out of the forest to the town of Pfaffikon and the congestion of Zuricher See.

An even less challenging pass called **Sattelegg,** 1130 meters, loops east from the north end of Ibergeregg back toward Zurich See and civilization. Sattelegg has a pleasant restaurant, but an unpleasantly low speed limit.

West of Andermatt

The Berner Oberland

West of Andermatt, west of the Furka and the Grimsel and the Susten, downstream from the Aareschlucht, in the valley of the Aare River, is the town of **Interlaken.** It's in canton Bern, in the area called the Berner Oberland, the high mountain country south of Switzerland's capital, Bern.

Interlaken is between two lakes made by the Aare River, the **Brienzer See** to the east and the **Thuner See,** to the west. It has been host to every guided tour that hits Switzerland. It's the jumping-off place for cog train rides up the Jungfrau mountain. It's also a great place to buy a Swiss army knife or a watch from Bucherer or a cup of genuine English tea. On one cross street into the old part of town, there's a hardware store (Eisenwaren) with everything from hand tools to Swiss cowbells. The saving grace of this tourist trap town is the public parking in front of most of the shops, and the good riding in the nearby mountains.

The area is crawling with hotels. There are big ones and little ones, expensive and cheap, in the bigger towns, on lakes, and hanging on the mountainside above little villages.

The island village of **Iseltwald,** one potential home base, hugs the cliffs on the south shore of Brienzer See. To get there, take the Autobahn around the south shore of the lake and take the exit (Ausfahrt) onto Iseltwald. Tourist Office; CH-3807 Iseltwald; phone: 033 845-1201.

A choice hotel right on the lake where the lake steamer stops is the **Strand Hotel;** CH-3807 Iseltwald; phone: 033 845-1313; fax: 033 845-1315. Upon exiting the freeway onto Iseltwald, there's a parking lot for tourists. The road into the village is marked with the international "do not enter" sign. But the little white sign underneath reads to the effect of, "unless you have business." So ride on in and have some business.

Another village with hotels, restaurants, and rooms for rent is **Beatenberg,** on the cliff hundreds of meters above the north shore of the Thuner See. Follow signs from the north side of Interlaken. From the whole village, there are sweeping views of Thuner See below and the Berner Oberland mountains beyond, including the Jungfrau. Beatenberg is a good place to catch Alpenglow, the almost hot pink glow of snow covered mountains in the rising or setting sun.

On the opposite shore of Brienzer See from Iseltwald is an outdoor museum called **Ballenberg** with a collection of farmhouses from all parts of Switzerland. They're furnished and have costumed people working in and around them. There are two entrances (and exits) a lower one near the town of Brienz, and a higher one about halfway up the **Brunig Pass.** Park and walk in.

A steam cog train climbs from Brienz to a mountaintop restaurant called Rothorn.

On the north bank of the Aare River in Interlaken is **Hotel Goldey;** CH-3800 Interlaken; phone: 033 822-4445; fax: 033 823-2345.

There's a small modern hotel just off the main drag in Interlaken, behind the post office and across a little plaza from the hardware store. **City Hotel;** CH-3800 Interlaken Am Marktplatz; phone: 033 822-1022; fax: 033 823-1018.

West of Interlaken, on the south shore of the Thuner See at CH-3705 Faulen See, is the **Strand Hotel Seeblick;** phone: 033 854-2321; fax: 033 854-2348.

Trip 5 Switzerland's Yosemite

Distance   *About 60 kilometers round trip from Interlaken*
Terrain   *Curving valley roads*
Highlights   *Spectacular cliffs, waterfalls, and glaciered mountains*
★

There's a dead-end valley 12 kilometers south of Interlaken so breathtakingly beautiful, such a joy to behold, that it's worth a detour. It's called **Lauterbrunnen,** valley of the

The Lauterbrunnen valley, known as the valley of the waterfalls—Switzerland's Yosemite—is located just a few kilometers from Interlaken. It is possible to stay right at the foot of Staubbach waterfall, shown here. The witch's hat church steeple is typical of German-speaking Switzerland. This is the countryside where all the tourists have fondue, some expressing surprise that it isn't always cheese.

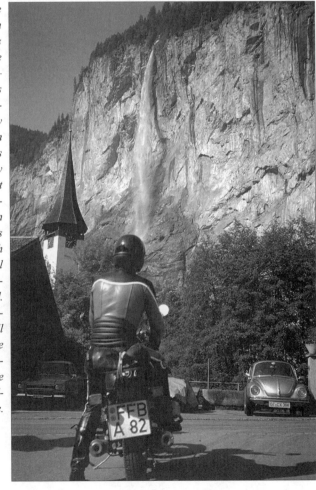

waterfalls. The valley is narrower than Yosemite, and has at least as many waterfalls, one inside the mountain, called **Trummelbach.** It's possible to stay in the valley. Two hotels are the **Schutzen;** phone: 033 855-2032; fax: 033 855-2950; and the **Jungfrau;** phone: 033 855-3434; fax: 033 855-2523; both addressed CH-3822 Lauterbrunnen. The latter has a good indoor pool.

A cable car from Lauterbrunnen goes up to the top of the Schilthorn mountain to what is reportedly the highest revolving restaurant in the world. You may have seen it in a James Bond film.

The road to Lauterbrunnen intersects with a road into the next valley east. It leads in just a few kilometers to the village of **Grindelwald.** Grindelwald is pretty touristy, but it's at the base of the **Eiger,** the mountain face that Clint Eastwood played on in the movie, *The Eiger Sanction.* It's handy to know that the Eiger, another word for "devil," is separated from the Jungfrau mountain, "the maiden," by a mountain called "Monk."

There are several villages with hotels above Lauterbrunnen and Grindelwald accessible only by cog train or cable car.

There are plenty of hotels in Grindelwald.

The Schallenberg is a non-commercial, non-tourist, motorcycle favorite. The cafe at the top has special parking for bikes and a prize second floor balcony from which to watch the developing scene below.

Trip 6 North of Interlaken

Distance	*About 180 kilometers from Interlaken via Glaubenberg Pass plus about 40 via Acherli Pass*
Terrain	*Sweeping and twisting through meadows and forests on five lower passes, some narrow, tight stuff*
Highlights	*Bucolic motorcycle favorite roads, a couple of motorcycle cafes, mostly off tourist routes, Schallenberg (1167 meters), ★Glaubenbuelen Pass (1611 meters), ★Glaubenberg Pass (1643 meters), Brunig Pass (1008 meters), ★Acherli Pass (1458 meters)*

This loop offers pleasant, bucolic, often challenging, but not exotic riding off the main tourist routes. Alpine guidebooks don't mention these roads.

The **Schallenberg** road starts climbing from the town of **Thun,** at the west end of the Thuner See, the westerly of the two lakes that bracket Interlaken. From the north side of Thun, signs direct you first to **Steffisburg,** then to Schallenberg. (The English ear doesn't distinguish between "burg" and "berg," but technically the former is a fortified town and the latter is a mountain.) Steffisburg is home to Motor Center Thun, a huge new BMW and Honda shop with rentals.

This is a sweeper road that has no great commercial or tourist value, so it's a motorcycle favorite. The area is a bit less polished-looking than most parts of Switzerland. The cafe at the top, Restaurant Gabelspitz, is almost exclusively aimed at serving *Tofflers.* All the close-by parking is for motorcycles. A choice second-floor balcony lets patrons watch the road and the parking lot activity.

The east side of the Schallenberg comes down to a village called **Wiggen.** From Wiggen, the trip heads east in the direction of Luzern for a few kilometers. Just at the edge of a town called **Schupfheim,** a road to the right leads south to a town called Fluhli. This is the **Glaubenbuelen Pass** road, sometimes called *Panorama Strasse.* From Fluhli, the road is twisting, paved, one-lane across the top with lovely views of lakes and mountains and forests. But it seems like only cows are looking at the panorama. There are no restaurants, no services. The Swiss will insist that Heidi came from eastern Switzerland, but the Glaubenbuelen looks like what Heidi country ought to look like. In the fall and spring the road may be full of cows heading to or from the high pastures, with floral headdresses in the fall. In either case, the lead cow will wear a big brass bell hung from an elaborate collar. Lesser cows have smaller bells and smaller collars, down to the least with tin sheet metal bells.

The pass road connects with the main highway between Interlaken and Luzern at **Giswil,** just in time to climb west over the Brunig Pass in the direction of Interlaken. (Looking for the Panorama Strasse from Giswil, the only hint is a sign on the main road pointing to Schupfheim. Look for the Giswil church which sits back on sort of a nob. The Panorama Strasse goes by it.)

To extend the trip, instead of going back to Interlaken over the Brunig, take the main road in the opposite direction toward Luzern. Then at **Sarnen,** head back north on the **Glaubenberg Pass.** More below.

The Brunig isn't high, but it *did* have some great sweepers that drew motorcycles from all around. A few years ago an avalanche took out most of the good sweepers and some vehicles with it. The replacement road does the job, but has less oomph. There remains one corner, a righthander going up from the east, that has a pull-out space that fills with bikes on good days. And the several restaurants and hotels at the top often host huge crowds of motorcyclists. Friday night is supposed to be *the* night on the Brunig. The **Motel Restaurant Brunig** always has a sport bike mounted on a post out front, changed from time to time. CH-6082 Brunig; phone: 033 971-1133. Across the road, the Restaurant Silvana has a big lot carved out of the mountainside, often packed with bikes. Its front tables are right on the road for good view and sound. From the top of the Brunig, a dead-end road goes south a few kilometers to some small villages with good views of the Aare valley, including **Meiringen** and Reichenbach Falls, described in Trip 1.

Parallel to and east of the Glaubenbuelen Pass (the *Panorama Strasse*) is another pass road called Glaubenberg. They must have named them to confuse us. Anyway, it's at least as high, even less used, and is also one-lane across the top. A restaurant/ski lodge named Hotel Langis on the south slope accommodates lots of motorcyclists during the summer. The north end of the Glaubenberg is in the middle of a village called **Entlebuch,** a few kilometers closer to Luzern than Schupfheim, above. Its southeast side ends at Sarnen, a town at the end of a lake by the same name.

From Sarnen it's possible to cross the main road and catch an obscure pass called **Acherli** over the next mountain into the Engelberg valley. There are no signs for the pass, so

Even though some of its famous sweepers were swept away by an avalanche, Brunig Pass has always been popular. The Motel Restaurant Brunig, atop the pass, is a "Tofftreftpunkt," a motorcycle meeting place.

follow the signs from Sarnen to Kerns and then to Sand. The only intersection in Sand is at the north edge of the village, and that's the pass road. Leaving Sand on the pass road there's a reassuring sign, "**Dallenwil,**" the next town in the Engelberg valley. A couple of kilometers in the woods above Sand are gravel. Across the top and down the south side is one-lane, paved, open cattle range. There are electric cattle gates. The winding road through green vistas is lovely. It comes out on the main street of Dallenwil. Coming the other way, from the Engelberg valley there are no signs for the pass either. Just follow the main road into and through Dallenwil.

From the Engelberg road it's only a few kilometers on the Autobahn toward the St. Gotthard to Beckenried, where a ferry crosses the Vierwaldstatter See to the Axenstrasse and the roads of Trip 4. There's a fine hotel restaurant right at the ferry with a terrace overlooking lake and mountains. **Sternen Hotel am See; CH-6375 Beckenried; phone: 041 64-1107.** Ferries run about once an hour. A less romantic connection from Beckenried to the roads of Trip 4 is the Autobahn tunnel, four lanes, about 5 kilometers through the cliffs above Vierwaldstatter See. A marvel, but no view.

Or head back over the Brunig Pass to Interlaken.

The west side of the Brunig has a connecting road to the Susten and Grimsel Passes, the roads of Trip 1. Weekend bikers often head that way.

On Thursday nights, thousands of motorcyclists gather for tire kicking at the Eisenbahn restaurant in the Swiss village of Trimbach bei Olten. Bikes fill the parking lot, and the rest spill over adjoining fields and roads.

Trip 7   Gurnigel

Distance	*About 120 kilometers, round trip from Interlaken*
Terrain	*Lakeside road, then a climb through woods to high pasture*
Highlights	*Handsome lakefront, woods, maybe military artillery, Gurnigel Pass (1608 meters)*

Riggisberg, about 15 kilometers northwest of the town of Thun, is the access key to a loop west of the Thuner See. From Riggisberg, this loop heads south on back roads to the summit at a restaurant called Berghaus Gurnigel. The easterly leg of the loop is a full two-lane road. The westerly leg is partly one-lane and is a bit rough, although paved. Both are fun. Both have good views, as does the restaurant at the top. The restaurant terrace has views over the low mountains to the south, often used for military exercises.

Trip 8   Trimbach bei Olten

Distance *About 140 kilometers, one way from Interlaken*

Terrain *Highway and Autobahn*

Highlights *Thousands and thousands of motorcycles*
★

Friday night is the meeting night on Brunig Pass, but the biggest gathering of riders is usually on Thursday night at **Trimbach bei Olten** (Trimbach is just north of Olten), about 80 kilometers straight north of Interlaken, south of Basel, and west of Zurich. To get to Trimbach bei Olten from Interlaken, head north over the Brunig Pass and continue on the Autobahn past Luzern. Olten is just off the Autobahn, about halfway between Luzern and Basel. Or take the Autobahn from Interlaken to Thun and Bern and then to Olten.

A huge parking lot next to a modest Gasthaus named Eisenbahn (railroad) accommodates about 3,000 motorcycles, and on good nights they spill out over neighboring fields. No events. No program. Only tire kicking. Special parking is reserved for any and all Harleys. The latest everything will show up, along with customized and restored bikes of all kinds. Every Thursday. Unfortunately, there aren't any recommended hotels nearby. There are a couple of serviceable ones in Olten.

▲▲ Leysin/Villars

•••

Hung on a mountainside at about 1200 meters, **Leysin** is a village with a view and a lot of hotels, and it's off the beaten track. It's in canton Vaud, and French, *s'il vous plait.* From most any point on the one road through town, from any balcony on any hotel, and from any terrace, there's a view across the Valley of the Rhone River (that started at the glacier on the Furka Pass) to the eternal snows of Mont Blanc and its neighbors.

Leysin is about six kilometers off the **Col des Mosses** road, the one road into Leysin, above the Rhone Valley town of **Aigle.** A cog train runs down the mountain from Leysin to Aigle.

A small family-run hotel near the top of the town, with views and good hearty cooking, is the **Hotel Mont Riant;** CH-1854 Leysin-Feydey; phone: 024 494-2701; fax: 024 494-2704.

Another is **Hotel Colina;** CH-1854 Leysin; phone: 024 493-3111; fax: 024 493-3199.

Since there's a Swiss hotel school in Leysin, there are many other hotels, some quaint and some more grand. In case you need a wash cloth, there's even a Holiday Inn.

An alternate to Leysin is **Villars,** a village hanging on an adjacent mountainside above Aigle at about 1200 meters. It's signed from Aigle and from **Bex** and is the jumping off place for the **Col de la Croix.** A good hotel bet is the international style **Eurotel;** CH-1884 Villars; phone: 024 435-3131; fax: 024 435-3953. There are many more modest.

Villars is home to a handy hotel guide for the budget traveler in Switzerland called E and G Hotels. "E" and "G" stand for Einfach and Gemutlich, which gets translated, "simple and cozy." It's published every year and lists about 175 or so modestly priced hotels all over Switzerland. Each listing has a color picture along with prices, hours, address, phone, and a clever symbol system that describes showers, pools, view, and other amenities. Naturally, a cheaper hotel in the city may prove less attractive than one of similar price in the country. The book is available at all Swiss tourist offices, or write **E and G Hotels,** Case Postal; CH-1844 Villars; phone: 024 495-1111; fax: 024 495-7514.

Trip 9 Simmen Tal and Jaun Pass

Distance	*About 145 kilometers from Interlaken to Leysin via Jaun Pass; about 110 kilometers via Saanenmoser*
Terrain	*Easy sweeping climbs over low passes*
Highlights	*Picturesque villages and covered bridges, lush pastures, forest, medieval walled town and famous cheese factory (Gruyeres), Jaun Pass (1509 meters), Saanenmoser (1279 meters)*

The picturesque Simmen Tal (valley) feeds into the south shore of the Thuner See, just west of Interlaken. From the lake, the road up the valley winds past quaint wooden covered bridges and through small villages. Unfortunately, it's marked "no passing" (double white, not double yellow) for practically its whole length. And the many little villages are famous for strict enforcement of speed limits.

Up the Simmen Tal about 15 kilometers from the Thuner See is a tiny one-building village called Weissenburg (don't confuse it with Weissenbach, farther upstream). The building is the **Hostellerie Alte Post** at Weissenburg, a joy for any antique connoisseur as well as anyone ready for a genuine Swiss meal. It's famous for serving coffee cream in chocolate cups that melt in the coffee.

The top of the Simmen Tal is called **Saanenmoser,** not much of a pass, but it leads right into one of Switzerland's classiest tourist areas: **Gstaad.** *Everybody* skis and tennises here, or at least the rich and famous are supposed to.

From Gstaad, it's straight over the **Col du Pillon** to Leysin, or from nearby **Saanen,** it's straight ahead over the Col des Mosses to Leysin. To Villars, take the Col du Pillon and Col de la Croix right into Villars. Both of these roads are more completely described in Trip 10. The road up the mountain to Leysin is just about where the Col du Pillon road and the Col des Mosses road meet.

But should you choose the longer route over the **Jaun Pass,** the turnoff is out in the country, in a meadow, just outside the little Simmen Tal village of Reidenbach. Jaun Pass (yawn, not whawn) runs between the Simmen Tal on the east and **Gruyeres** on the west with views of the Simmen Tal. It's an easy climb and there's a restaurant at the top of the pass.

Gruyeres, on the west end of the Jaun Pass, is a preserved old walled city on a hill. No vehicles. It's worth the short walk in to visit. Bikes can park right by the city gate. Too many restaurants offer almost any concoction or most any kind of berry with the thickest, richest cream imaginable, cream that comes from the cheese factory for which the town is known. On through plaza and shops of the walled village is a castle, for which an entry fee is charged. The factory is at the bottom of the hill and is open to visitors in the morning. Do the town rather than the cheese. In case you hadn't guessed, Gruyeres is French speaking.

South from Gruyeres is the Col des Mosses, leading to the road to Leysin, or on to Aigle and Villars.

Trip 10 Three Cols and a Route

Distance	*About 144 kilometers from Leysin*
Terrain	*Fun sweepers over lower passes, mostly modern highways, modest height and difficulty*
Highlights	*Well known resorts (Gstaad, Chateau d'Oex), log village (Saanen), German/French culture border, Col du Pillon (1546 meters), ★ Col de la Croix (1778 meters), Col des Mosses (1445 meters), Route Militaire*

The Col des Mosses climbs out of the Rhone Valley from Aigle, past a handsome private castle, and past the dead-end road to Leysin.

Chateau d'Oex (sounds like "shat oh decks") and Rougemont are attractive tourist towns at the north end of the Col des Mosses. The highway now bypasses both villages. The medieval church at Rougemont is worth a stop if you're passing by. Although the village is French speaking, the church is of Germanic style, because the diocese was controlled from nearby Germanic Saanen.

Rougemont has a comfortable log hotel restaurant called Hotel de Commune.

An interesting and fun alternate route parallels the Col des Mosses from Aigle. It's a military road and is open only on Saturdays, Sundays, and holidays. The south end, out of the valley village of Corbeyrier climbs through handsome vineyards, then some narrow, steep hairpins and a twisting, one-way-at-a-time tunnel.

The north end cruises by a lake, then over many bridges. Some pass roads number the hairpins. This one numbers the bridges: forty some. Unfortunately, part of the road has a low speed limit.

At the lovely log house village of Saanen (also the westerly base of the Sannenmoser) the road heads south for Gstaad, and then starts climbing the Col du Pillon through the village of **Gsteig,** which has one of the nicer Germanic-Swiss church steeples, shaped much like a witch's hat.

As the name Col du Pillon implies, the top of the pass is in French-speaking Switzerland. In the few kilometers between Gsteig and the top of the pass, the buildings and menus change from Germanic to French.

The attractive restaurant at the top of the Col du Pillon, with a terrace viewing the highest peaks in the area, is called Les Diablerets. So are the peaks. So is the next town. At the next town, Les Diablerets, the Col de la Croix road heads southwest. Somehow, the Col de la Croix is uncluttered, with sweeping turns and sweeping views. It has gotten rough in spots. The Col road comes down to the village of Villars, one of the few Swiss towns that's anxious to sell condos to foreigners.

At Villars, the road forks. One leg heads for the Rhone Valley at Aigle. One winds down to the valley at Bex. From either, it's just a few kilometers back up the Col des Mosses road to Leysin.

Cobblestones like these remain only on short historic pieces of road. These cobblestones help preserve the atmosphere in front of the Castle of Chillon on Lac Leman (Lake Geneva). The castle was made famous in English literature by Lord Byron's poem, The Prisoner of Chillon. *The nearby autoroute (freeway) is fast and smooth.*

Trip 11 The Swiss Jura

Distance *About 390 kilometers round trip from Leysin or Villars, about half on autoroute (freeway), about 200 kilometers from or to Col de la Faucille*

Terrain *Some autoroute, farm land, lower wooded passes with narrow, non-tourist roads, French culture*

Highlights *Good views of Lac Leman, Lac du Joux, Lac du Neuchatel, famous Castle of Chillon, Col du Mollendruz (1180 meters), Col de Marchairuz (1447 meters), ★Col de l'Aiguillon (1293 meters), Col des Etroits (1152 meters), Vue des Alpes (1283 meters), Col du Chasseral (1502 meters, toll), Weissenstein (1279 meters), Col du Mont Crosin (1227 meters)*

The Jura is a range of mountains just northwest of Lac Leman and the lower Rhone River. About half the Jura are in the French-speaking part of Switzerland and half are in France. They're pretty mellow compared to the rugged Alps, more like the Smokies in the U.S. This trip covers all the good riding in the Swiss Jura, all reachable from the Leysin/Villars base. The French Jura are in Trip 16.

Or maybe stay at a spectacularly sited mid-point hotel, La Mainaz, just in France at the Swiss border, high in the Jura overlooking **Lac Leman** and **Geneve.** From the hotel room, you can see all of Geneve, the Jet d'Eau, a major portion of the lake, and beyond that, **Mount Blanc** itself. The hotel is all by itself on the **Col de la Faucille,** just twenty minutes from the Geneve airport. On one side of the hotel are the Swiss Jura, the French on the other. **La Mainaz,** Route Nationale 5, La Faucille; F-01170 Gex; phone: 045 041-3110; fax: 045 041-3177. It's a Relais de Silence . . . a quiet hotel, but motorcyclists have enjoyed it.

Arcing west from Leysin and Aigle for about 100 kilometers, the north shore of Lac Leman harbors the major cities of French-speaking Switzerland: **Montreux,** Lausanne, and at the west end, Geneve (Geneva). Suspended above the lake, sometimes on spectacular viaducts, an autoroute (freeway) whisks right by the **Castle of Chillon** (made famous by Lord Byron's poem) on the east end of the lake to Geneva on the west end.

The Castle of Chillon is a real medieval castle that seems to rise right out of Lac Leman. It can be visited and it's accessible from the lake shore road below the autoroute, just east of the city of Montreux.

To get to these passes, it's best to avoid traffic along the lake shore road by taking the autoroute west toward Geneve (Geneva), past Lausanne, exiting at **Aubonne,** then climbing northwest over the **Col de Marchairuz.** The restaurant atop Marchairuz has a hand washing machine. It's been in place for years yet seems unique. Put your hands in the opening. First warm water. Then soap. Then more warm water. Then warm air.

North of the col, the road descends to the **Lac du Joux.**

Follow the lake shore east, then up the low **Col du Mollendruz.** Just across the top head east to **Orbe,** then northeast to **Baulmes,** a pleasant small village nestled in a nook of the mountains. Into and through Baulmes is the **Col de l'Aiguillon** road. It climbs through forests and into meadows, a little road where no tourist has gone . . . at least not many. It meets a more main highway near the French border. Go east, staying in Switzerland, over the **Col des Etroits** to a town called **St. Croix,** then on east to **La Chaux de Fonds,** where a jaunt south goes over the **Vue des Alpes,** then merge with the autoroute to **Neuchatel** and follow the autoroute east under (that's right, under) the city of Neuchatel exiting at **La Neuveville** beside **Bieler See.** Climb north over the toll pass, **Col du Chasseral,** through **St. Imier,** and on northeast over the **Col du Mont Crosin,** then east toward Moutier. Just past **Court,** continue east to **Gansbrunner,** over a mountain called Binzberg in German and Graitery in French. At Gansbrunner, head south over **Weissenstein.** (Or cross the same mountain on the narrow Balmberg road a few kilometers further east at Welshenrohr. No tourists for sure.) From Solothurn, it's Autobahn back to Leysin/Villars.

Mont Blanc Region

The **Rhone Valley** makes a 90-degree bend at a pretty good sized Swiss town called **Martigny.** Quite French. It's where two pass roads head out to encircle the eternal snows of the highest mountain in the Alps, **Mont Blanc,** 4807 meters (15779 feet!). From Martigny the **Col de la Forclaz** road heads toward France, and the **Grand St. Bernard** road heads toward Italy.

Martigny, or any of the villages hung on the mountains around it, are good bases for the Mont Blanc trip. Right where the two pass roads come together in Martigny is a hotel called **La Porte d'Octodure;** CH-1921 Martigny-Croix; phone: 027 722-7121; fax: 027 722-2173. *Malhereusement,* it's a Best Western!

A little village called Les Marecottes, atop a spectacular road just eight kilometers from the Martigny town square, has a variety of hotels that have served motorcyclists well. Go northwest from the square, over a covered wooden bridge, and keep climbing. The road climbs a traverse overlooking the Rhone Valley, then crosses to the north side of the Gorge du Trient on a high bridge. From that point on, the road barely hangs on the cliff edge overlooking the gorge. A train up the gorge goes through to France. The road doesn't. Les Marecottes is near the end of the road. One hotel is called **Aux Mille Etoiles;** CH-1923 Les Marecottes; phone: 027 761-1665; fax: 027 761-1600.

From the autoroute in the Rhone Valley, the pass roads are signed via a bypass road that misses downtown Martigny.

The trips in this chapter are accessible from Leysin or Villars.

Trip 12   Valley of the Rhone

Distance   *About 160 kilometers between Martigny and Andermatt, one way; about 110 kilometers between Martigny and Tasch (Zermatt), one way; about 100 kilometers between Martigny and Simplon Pass, one way*

Terrain   *Fairly straight valley road and sweeping mountain climbs on good modern highway*

Highlights   *Sweep up a finger valley toward the Matterhorn, over a high mountain pass (★ Simplon, at 2006 meters), some concrete roofed highway*

From the high passes at Andermatt, the Rhone Valley makes a pretty straight shot down to Martigny. The higher eastern part of the valley, called the Goms, is an amusing ride through log cabin villages. The lower part is more commercial and boring. It does make a functional east-west connection, about 150 kilometers long, with such high mountains on both sides that there's hardly any way out. From the Grimsel Pass back by Andermatt, there's no through road going north until the Col des Mosses by Leysin. It is possible to put a bike or car on a train and take it through a tunnel toward Interlaken. Switzerland is slowly extending an Autobahn autoroute up the valley.

Two dead-end roads north make for interesting escapes into high valleys: **Lotschen Tal** climbs up to the glaciers behind Lauterbrunnen (turn off at the signs for the train tunnel to Goppenstein), and the **Col du Sanetsch** from **Sion** almost makes it across the top to Gsteig, but doesn't.

One road out of the Rhone Valley to the south toward Italy, the **Simplon Pass,** starts at **Brig,** 50 kilometers below the Furka. The Simplon is one of the major passes of the Alps between Italy and France, through Switzerland. The first major Alpine train tunnel went under the Simplon to carry the Orient Express. Both sides of the pass road are in Switzerland, with good quality sweepers to the summit on both sides. The north side has an amazing "S" curved poured concrete suspension bridge. On the summit is a giant stone eagle monument and a couple of serviceable restaurants. One regular menu item is goulash soup, a spicy, meaty specialty of the Germanic Alps that tastes something like chili.

Near Brig, there's a fairly good sized bike shop in the adjoining village of Naters, right beside the road east toward the Furka.

(For good road connections from the south side of the Simplon, see Trip 23, "Simplon Pass")

Several dead-end valleys go south from the Rhone Valley. The most famous valley is **Matter Tal** to **Zermatt** and the **Matterhorn,** but no vehicles are allowed into Zermatt. The Rhone Valley turnoff for Zermatt and the Matter Tal is at **Visp.** It's a fine sweeping ride up the Matter Tal as far as **Tasch,** where one of the biggest parking lots in Europe accommodates tourists taking the cog train the rest of the way to Zermatt. There is underground and indoor parking at Tasch. Outdoor bike parking is available right next to the train station.

The village of Randa, just below Tasch, bears witness to the terror of the Alps. In recent years a whole mountain collapsed into the valley, burying everything—the stream, parts of the village, the road and railroad—under granite boulders. The road and railroad now go around the site.

The east fork of the intersection in the road up the Matter Tal goes all the way up to the towns of Saas Fee and **Saas Almagell.** The road to the former is interesting, with glaciers right at hand, but it's a walk-around-only village. Motorcycle parking is free.

Just downstream from Visp in the Rhone Valley, without a sign, everything changes from German to French: architecture, menus, bread, even cars.

Sion is a large city with motorcycle shops that speak French. Visible from the valley road near Sion are military airplane hangars in the mountainside and airstrips alongside the road.

From the Swiss side of the Col du Grand St. Bernard, the restaurant in sunny Italy is almost at hand. Across the border in those buildings there will be cappucino and fresh pasta.

Trip 13 All Around Mont Blanc

* *

Distance   *About 300 kilometers from Martigny*

Terrain   *Circle the greatest mountain in the Alps, Mont Blanc; from low valleys with some congestion, climb to empty mountain roads; three major Alpine passes and several lesser ones; some narrow, tight, steep hairpins*

Highlights   *Three countries, famous passes and ski resorts, Roman ruins, plus some quiet, remote, twisting stuff, Champex, ★ Col du Grand St. Bernard (2469 meters), ★Colle San Carlo (1971 meters), ★Col du Petit St. Bernard (2188 meters), ★ ★ Cormet de Roselend (1922 meters), ★Col du Pre (1703 meters), Col des Saisies (1633 meters), Chamonix, Col des Montets (1461 meters), Col de la Forclaz (1526 meters), Col des Planches (1411 meters), Col du Lein (1656 meters), Champex (1486 meters)*

Three amusing little roads start near Martigny. Just toward downtown a few hundred meters from the Hotel La Porte d'Octodure, a tiny road, the **Col des Planches,** climbs up the mountainside. It isn't high, but it does lead up and over to a high resort at Verbier, 1390 meters. Up the Grand St. Bernard a few kilometers, at Les Valettes, another small road makes a twisting climb up to a mountain lake village called **Champex.** The road goes through and winds back down to the Grand St. Bernard road at Orsieres, where an interesting dead-end valley road, Val Ferret, heads up toward some glaciers at 1705 meters.

The third amusing little road is the **Col du Lein,** crossing the mountain behind Martigny between **Saxon** in the Rhone Valley and the Grand St. Bernard road near Sembrancher. Saxon is about ten kilometers east of Martigny, and the turnoff is from the center of the village, marked Col du Len, not Lien. Sembrancher is twelve kilometers up the Grand St. Bernard road from Martigny. The little col road climbs to about 1000 meters, one lane, with about four kilometers unpaved.

There are two St. Bernard Passes, a Grand (big) and a Petit or Piccolo (little) St. Bernard. The big one goes between Martigny, Switzerland, and **Aosta,** Italy. It's where the dogs are. The little one goes from Aosta in Italy to France. There's a statue of St. Bernard on both of them.

The Grand St. Bernard Pass is fairly commercial and has high-speed sweepers so well engineered that it's hard to realize how quickly you're up among the glaciers. But it goes by tunnel into Italy. Motorcycles want to stay on the pass road, so turn off just after entering the tunnel, where a sign, "Col," points to the right. At the top, the restaurant on the Italian side is more pleasant than the Swiss one. Sometimes the col is labeled "ouvert," open, on the Swiss side, but the border crossing just over the col is closed. Sometimes it's closed with huge concrete blocks. The Swiss one will have sandwiches and cold cuts; the Italian, fresh pasta and salad and cappuccino. Most of the dogs around are stuffed toys. On the Italian side, the 14 kilometers between the pass and the Italian entrance to the tunnel are fairly challenging and wild. Approaching the pass from Italy, the pass road leaves the tunnel road just before a long viaduct that leads to the tunnel entrance. There's a place to change money at the complex of offices just across the viaduct. Italian lira are needed for cash purchases in Italy. The rest of the route down into Aosta has commercial traffic.

Aosta center has some significant **Roman ruins,** an arch, walls, and a theater. On the east end of town, past the airport,

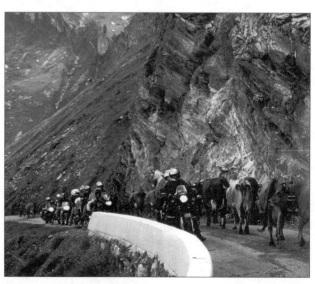

Beaufort cheese on the hoof, high on the Cormet de Roselend, one of France's over-looked passes. Cows use the road to reach high pastures in the spring, and to come down in the fall. You'll know if you come up behind them, as they leave a well marked trail.

is a very large motorcycle shop called America. It does not sell Harleys. It does fit tires quickly.

Even though it's in a fabulous Alpine valley, Aosta has a lot of traffic and smog, alleviated recently by the newly completed Monte Bianco autostrada that bypasses the town taking most trucks and busses with it.

There is a serviceable hotel in Aosta. **Hotel Valle d'Aosta** is on the east end of town, I-11100 Aosta; phone: 01 655-1845; fax: 01 65 233-6660. (See Trip 14 for riding in the vicinity of Aosta).

To get to the **Piccolo St. Bernard Pass** from Aosta, follow the signs to Courmayeur and the Italian entrance to what used to be the longest vehicle tunnel in the world under Mont Blanc. Commercial truck traffic to the tunnel is terrible. An elaborate autostrada is under construction, but . . . . Fortunately, motorcyclists need not go through the tunnel. From the smog-filled highway there are occasional glimpses of Mont Blanc, huge and white, before the turnoff at the village of **Pre St. Didier,** 30 kilometers from Aosta, where the Piccolo St. Bernard goes south and leaves the traffic behind.

Or better yet, before the Piccolo St. Bernard turnoff at Pre St. Didier, there's a long cut over an obscure pass called the **Colle San Carlo.** It's recently been improved with new retaining walls and pavement. Escape the traffic early by turning up the Colle at a village called **Morgex.** The pass isn't marked. The sign is to Arpy, a town on the pass. After a great climb twisting through the forests, the road descends into the village of **La Thuile,** on the Piccolo St. Bernard road.

The rest of the Italian side of the Piccolo St. Bernard is a delight. Often the road cuts through deep banks of snow well into mid-June. The only village, La Thuile, has a good ristorante called Grotto, and another called Les Marmottes just across from the little and only parking lot in town. Try tortellini carne in garlic and walnut sauce.

Sometimes on the Piccolo St. Bernard there is nobody around to check traffic out of Italy or into France, and no place to change money. Banks at **Bourg St. Maurice,** the closest town of note in France, close at noon. Fortunately, the only restaurants, on the French side, will usually take Swiss or French francs or Italian lira. And even remote gas stations and restaurants in France take credit cards.

Some American motorcyclists have noted that French road repair crews use a lot of gravel, often marked with a portable sign that profiles a pre-World War II Citroen spraying rocks from its wheels. Gravel piles can spoil the French side of the Grand St. Bernard.

One of the *plus joli* (prettiest) roads in France, the **Cormet de Roselend** (sounds like "core may"), starts at Bourg St. Maurice at the base of the Petit (it's *petit* in France, not *piccolo*) St. Bernard. Find it heading north from the east end of town. The road has no commercial or even ski activity. Early in the season, it may be marked *ferme* (closed) because of snow. Give it a try. Very possibly a bike can get through. Parts are only one lane wide and bumpy, but it feels like no one else was ever there. Near the top should be herds of handsome red-brown cows, source of the famous cheese that comes from the other side of the mountain at Beaufort.

On the north side of the Cormet is a beautiful lake with a couple of satisfactory mountain restaurants. The northerly one is a bit more substantial in building and menu. The lake results from a dam (*barrage* in French) with a road across the top that leads to another pass of no significance except views so wonderful that even the most enthusiastic rider will pause to look. It's mostly one lane wide, paved, and is called **Col du Pre.** There is a restaurant on it. Then, it winds down into the town of cheese, Beaufort.

Three kilometers below Beaufort the **Col des Saisies** (sounds like "coal day sigh zee") road comes in. Cross country skiing events for the Albertville Olympics were held at the Col des Saisies. It's a north/south pass, with the north end daylighting at **Flumet,** a little village on a valley road that leads toward Megeve and **Chamonix.**

But wait, there's a more fun and more beautiful way up the Col des Saisies. The signed road three kilometers down from Beaufort heads up a finger valley in the direction of Hauteluce. But just one kilometer further downstream is a sign for a village, Villard. Go into Villard, and keep climbing, back and forth switchbacks up the face of the mountain with views for miles and kilometers. The road eventually makes it up to the col and joins the main road. Just across the col, at a mini-traffic circle, there should be a sign for Crest Voland, a little village down on the edge of the mountain. It's a fun alternative to the main road into Flumet.

Coming into Chamonix, all traffic gets funneled onto an autoroute that marches up the valley on stilts out over the top of everything. Finally, at Chamonix, the huge glaciers of Mont Blanc come into view. And the tunnel entrance to Italy. Chamonix is a summer and winter tourist center with all the accommodations and traffic to prove it. One of the most exotic cable car rides (*telepherique* in French) in the world goes from Chamonix to the Aiguille du Midi on the Mont Blanc massif. From the main highway through the city, an underpass takes you to the parking lot of the cable car. The ride up is exciting if the weather's clear.

Most of the traffic is going through the tunnel to Italy, not to Switzerland. For Switzerland, follow the signs to Argentiere and Col des Montets, a hardly noticeable pass, and on to the Swiss border.

The Swiss side of the border crossing has all kinds of services, including money exchanges. Across the border there's a turnoff to a town called Finhaut. A road climbs through Finhaut to dead-end at a lake called Emosson at 1930 meters. The road's good and there's a restaurant with a terrace and view of the whole Mont Blanc massif.

Back at the foot of the mountain, the road on to Martigny climbs over the **Col de la Forclaz.** The Martigny side of this col has a couple of restaurants with good views of the Rhone Valley and surrounding vineyards.

Trip 14 Val d'Aosta

Distance	*About 78 kilometers from Martigny to Aosta, one way, plus about 50 kilometers from Aosta to Breuil (the Matterhorn, called Monte Cervino in Italy) one way, plus about 25 kilometers from Aosta to any of the valleys in the Parco Nazionale Gran Paradiso, one way*
Terrain	*Once out of the Aosta valley, quiet, twisting narrow roads into high forgotten valleys surrounded by glaciers*
Highlights	*As close to the Matterhorn as a road goes, plus a natural National Park of glaciers and mountain peaks, ★Col di Joux (1640 meters)*

Just west of Aosta, on the traffic-jammed highway to Courmayeur (the Mont Blanc tunnel), three roads dead-end south
into the **Parco Nazionale Gran Paradiso.** The closest to
Aosta is **Val di Cogne,** the next is Val Savaranche, and the
third, Val di Rhemes. They quickly leave traffic and civilization behind. Each twists and climbs into high Alpine valleys.

Val di Cogne is a good base for hikers and climbers and
offers beautiful views of Mont Blanc and the Gran Paradiso.

Twenty-six kilometers from Aosta, going east on the
autostrada toward Torino, at **Chatillon,** a road climbs north

to 2006 meters and the very base of the Matterhorn. Of course, in Italia, it's **Monte Cervino.** The village at the base, **Breuil,** has a lot of ski hotels, usually closed in the summer.

Just short of the end of the road is a little lake, **Lago Bleu.** Climb up over a little slope to see a picture to treasure . . . . Cervino reflected in the lake.

Just downstream from Chatillon is a good pass road that makes an interesting loop, the **Col di Joux.** It climbs east from St. Vincent to the next valley where a lower col road loops back to St. Vincent and the autostrada. The col road is signed from the autostrada. Just west of the top of the Col di Joux is a restaurant with views to die for . . . the whole Aosta Valley west to Mont Blanc. The owner studied English in Buffalo!

The back side of the Matterhorn, the Italian side, where it's known as Monte Cervino, is best viewed across little Lago Bleu at Breuil.

Lac d'Annecy

In France, south of Mont Blanc, are some of the highest passes and wildest country of the Alps. Exciting to explore. The '92 Olympics at Albertville highlighted some of them. France alone of the Alpine countries has good, prominently marked route numbers.

Although they're pretty well developed for winter sports, the French Alps seem to close down during the summer season. Facilities, almost endless in number and variety elsewhere in the Alps, are a bit harder to locate in France, and some pass roads aren't open until late in June.

But facilities are always open at **Lac d'Annecy,** one of the loveliest lakes in the Alps, just a few kilometers northwest of Albertville. Passes south of Lac Leman lead to **Annecy,** as do the autoroutes south from Geneve and west from Chamonix. The French province that includes Annecy and most of these good passes is Haute Savoie. Its flag looks almost like the Swiss flag, a white cross on red. On Savoie's flag, the white arms of the cross reach the edge of the flag.

The town of Annecy, at the north end of the lake, has all services, including a variety of large and helpful motorcycle shops, even Harley. (Several are on the road to Aix les Bains.) Annecy has a colorful walking old town with little canals, and a smart modern lake front promenade and beach. The whole city presents a very clean, neat, pleasing aspect.

Hotels for all tastes are located around the lake. On the eastern shore is a village called **Talloires** (say "Tal whar"). Besides some starred (by Michelin) and pricey places like **George Bise** and **Le Cottage;** F-74290 Talloires; phone: 045 060-7110; there's **Hotel le Lac;** F-74290 Talloires; fairly pretentious; phone: 045 060-7108; fax: 045 060-7299. The owner is a biker and he also owns a ski hotel high in the Val d'Isere. Next door is the **Hotel la Charpenterie;** attractive and more modest; phone: 045 060-7047; fax: 045 060-7907; and **Hotel Beau Site;** phone: 045 060-7104.

Trip 15   Lac d'Annecy

• •

Distance	*About 230 kilometers from Martigny to Annecy, one way*
Terrain	*Sweeping and twisting over seven non-commercial passes*
Highlights	*Farms, forests, high meadows, some narrow roads, ski resorts, Pas de Morgins (1369 meters), Col du Corbier (1237 meters), Col des Gets (1163 meters), ★Col de Joux Plane (1712 meters), Col de la Colombiere (1613 meters), Col des Aravis (1486 meters), Col de la Croix Fry (1467 meters), Col de Joux Verte (1760 meters)*

Several passes south of Lac Leman make a fun connection with Annecy and the roads of the French Alps. On most of them there is no traffic. Start out of the Rhone Valley in Switzerland on the **Pas de Morgins.** From the town of **Monthey,** just a few kilometers downstream from Martigny, it climbs through pleasant Swiss countryside and crosses into France at the top. The operator of the motorcycle shop in Monthey is an enthusiast who has biked all over the world, including North America and Baja.

Coming down into France below the town of **Abondance,** the little pass road of **Col du Corbier** heads up and south into a wonderful set of switchbacks on the northeast side. It leads to the next valley and the road up the **Col des Gets.** To the east of Gets is another little pass road called **Col de Joux Plane.** It's a one-lane road that twists up from the town of Morzine on the north to Samoens on the south. It's not conspicuously marked at either end, but it's popular with French and Swiss motorcyclists and is worth the effort to find it. There is a restaurant at the top.

A high loop out of Morzine to Super Morzine (that's its name) climbs easterly to the **Col de Joux Verte** at 1760 meters and comes down at Montriond about five kilometers downstream from Morzine where it started. The northerly leg is through rustic country.

The whole loop adds about thirty kilometers.

This leads down to a fairly large city, **Cluses,** on the autoroute to Chamonix. Signing through Cluses is circuitous.

Across the autoroute from Cluses, the **Col de la Colombiere** leads up and over the mountains toward Annecy through St. Jean de Sixt and Thones. Colombiere is a non-commercial play road. Oil spills have been noted, though.

Col de Joux Plane, a narrow, obscure, fun pass in France, attracts a gathering of Harley riders. It is not well marked, but is worth finding.

There is a restaurant at the top.

From **Flumet,** on the loop around Mont Blanc (north end of the Col des Saisies (Trip 13), the **Col des Aravis** (say are uh VEE) goes up and over toward Annecy. The Col des Aravis has a nice restaurant with a terrace view of Mont Blanc. Just down a little on the north side of the Col des Aravis, near the ski resort of **la Clusaz,** the **Col de la Croix Fry** heads up and west. It's a good road with little traffic, and a nice hotel restaurant complex on the west slope named after the pass, **La Croix Fry;** F-74230 Manigod; phone: 045 044-9016; fax: 045 044-9028. The hotel has an outdoor pool. The Col de la Croix Fry leads to the town of Thones, and the main road to Annecy. A short cut to Talloires turns south at Bluffy.

Trip 16 The French Jura

• •

Distance	*About 210 kilometers from Annecy to Col de la Faucille, one way*
Terrain	*Mostly small rural roads, some rough, pleasant mountain vistas*
Highlights	*Walk in gorge, Grand Colombier (1531 meters), Col de la Faucille (1320 meters), Col de la Givrine (1229 meters), Col de Richemond (1060 meters)*

Just west of Annecy (and the autoroute) through **Lovagny** are the Gorges du Fier and a fine looking castle named Montrottier. You can park and walk through the gorge, not the castle.

Continue on across the Rhone Valley to **Culoz,** and climb the steep ascent of the **Montagne du Grand Colombier.** There's a rustic restaurant near the top at about 1500 meters, l'Auberge Le Grand Colombier, with a view southerly over the Lac du Bourget.

Wander along the Grand Colombier, northerly through **Brenaz,** and over the **Col de Richemond** which has a marker explaining that the col is named for World War II resistance martyrs.

Continue north across the autoroute near **Bellegarde,** where there are signs for **Col de la Faucille.** Climb a pleasant long valley then jog through some woods over the Col de la Faucille (1320 meters). (See Trip 11 for Hotel La Mainaz, dramatically sited on the col.) Geneve, Lac Leman, Swiss autoroutes are just over the col.

An alternate route, just before the Col de Faucille, is to turn north, crossing into Switzerland after a couple of kilometers over the **Col de la Givrine** (1229 meters). The col road and the border crossing meet in a triangle, but you have to go around two sides of it to get across the border.

To continue in the Swiss Jura, see Trip 11.

Trip 17   South of Lac D'Annecy

••

Distance   *About 250 kilometers round trip from Annecy*

Terrain   *From commercial valleys to mountain highs on every kind of
                paved road, limited facilities*

Highlights *Ski resorts, one of the highest and loneliest roads of the Alps ★ ★
                Col de l'Iseran, 2769 meters, Cret de Chatillon (1699 meters),
                Col de la Forclaz (1150 meters), ★ Col de la Madeleine (1984
                meters), Col du Glandon (1951 meters), Col de la Croix de Fer
                (2068 meters), Col de Tamie (902 meters)*

Some of the highest and most awesome passes of the Alps are
south of Albertville, but their lower slopes are less forested
and the heights seem grayer. In fact, they are often called the
Gray Alps. Civilization seems further removed.

In addition to the main highways linking Lac d'Annecy with Albertville to its south, it's possible to take one of several low but interesting passes. **Col de la Forclaz** (same name as the pass out of Martigny, Switzerland) climbs right up the mountainside out of Talloires. In just a few kilometers, the restaurants at the summit provide views of the lake and of Talloires far below, as well as lunch, hang gliding, and parasailing.

Across the lake, the **Cret de Chatillon** climbs right out of Annecy. In seconds the road is out of traffic and in the woods. Above the woods there is a restaurant terrace with views across the lake to Mont Blanc. The **Col de Tamie** connects the south end of the lake out of downtown Faverges with the roads south of Albertville.

The **Col de l'Iseran,** named after the Isere River and its valley, the Val d'Isere (the river is L'Isere in French, so it sounds like "lee zayer," and the pass sounds like "coal duh lee zay RAHN"), is one of the highest in the Alps. The valley is where all the skiing events took place in the Albertville Olympics. The col connects the upper reaches of the Val d'Isere with the next valley south, the Val d'Arc which sort of parallels it. Both flow to the Rhone. To reach the pass from Albertville, either follow the river upstream or take the scenic high-cut route over the Cormet de Roselend to Bourg St. Maurice and Seez, and on up the valley. The valley from Albertville is sort of a truck route, relieved somewhat by the autoroute built for the Olympics.

The ski center at Val d'Isere, about 86 kilometers from Albertville, looks naked and uninviting in the summer, with its concrete high rises set in big gravel parking lots, and most everything closed down. Above the ski center though, the road climbs and climbs through beautiful and ever-wilder looking country. As the deep snows melt in the early summer, the meadows are carpeted with flowers.

Cross the col and follow down the Arc, looking even starker and wilder, down as far as **St. Jean de Maurienne.** (For routes connecting farther south, see Trip 18.) Turn south and climb up the twisty **Col de la Croix de Fer,** which bends west and meets the **Col du Glandon.** There's a small restaurant atop the Croix de Fer with views of gray granite peaks and a long valley with a little village.

Head back north on the Col de Glandon road to the Arc valley at La Chambre. Just cross the main valley road and head up north on the Col de la Madeleine. The south side of the Col de la Madeleine is fairly modern alignment with ski resorts. There's a restaurant at the top. The north side is narrow and more rugged. A good lunch stop on the north side is the Hotel du Grand Pic at a village called Celliers, at about 1300 meters. Near the north end of the Col de Madeleine, almost back in the Val d'Isere there's a village quaintly named Pussy. It's not far back to Albertville and Lac d'Annecy. The Col de Tamie makes a good connection, bypassing Albertville.

The Southern Alps

A succession of kings and emperors pushed the French border east across the southern Alps at the expense of Italy, so that much of the high country is in France today. A few minor passes cross down into Italy. The countryside is bleak and the few towns are walled fortresses, left over from the defense budgets of past centuries. Here are some of the highest passes in the Alps, several of which are known today as the Route des Grandes Alpes. The first Napoleon is supposed to have come this route when he landed in France from exile on the Mediterranean island of Elba. Taking these highest roads, he escaped detection until he was ready to pounce on Paris. It must have been quite a trip in 1815. We know that 100 days later, he was defeated at Waterloo and got shipped off a bit farther than Elba.

While the northern Alps abound in tourist accommodations, restaurants and hotels are few and far between in the southern Alps, and often closed. The small village of **Guillestre,** at 1000 meters, offers the best amenities. It's one of those fortress towns with stone works that boggle the mind, left over from Louis XIV. Guillestre is south of **Briancon** and east of Gap, and the base of two passes on the Route des Grandes Alpes, the **Col de Vars** and the **Col d'Izoard. Les Barnieres** is a good modern hotel with a good restaurant, even tennis and a pool in season; F-05600 Guillestre; phone: 049 245-00507 or 049 245-0487. No English!

Why not stay at the highest hotel in the highest village in the Alps? Upstream, east of Guillestre, in the Parc Regional du Queyras, is a rustically preserved village called **St. Veran** at 2257 meters. At the village limits is a "no vehicles" sign, except those on business. You have business. Past the little village church there should be a sign pointing up to the **Chateau Renard** above the village; F-05350 St. Veran; Haute Alpes; phone: 049 245-8543; fax: 049 245-8420. English spoken. The owner's wife is from Tasmania. To get to St.

Veran, head up the Col d'Izoard, and turn east at the fortress, **Chateau Queyras.** A couple of kilometers past the fortress, turn south to **Molines** and then St. Veran. (See road description for Trip 19.)

Trip 18   Around Guillestre

....

Distance   *About 250 kilometers*

Terrain   *High, rugged mountains and roads, limited facilities*

Highlights   *Exotic wild scenery, ★ ★Col d'Izoard (2361 meters), Col de Montgenevre (1850 meters), into Italy, Sestriere (2033 meters), Col de Finestre (2174 meters), Col du Mt. Cenis (2083 meters), Col du Telegraphe (1578 meters), ★ ★Col du Galibier (2645 meters), Col du Lautaret (2058 meters), Col de Montgenevre (1850 meters)*

East from Guillestre the Col d'Izoard road enters the Parc Regional du Queyras following the gorge of the Guil river. The road twists and tunnels through the gorge (this part of the road often seems to have gravel on it, not always conveniently placed) and climbs to a fork at a fortress on a mountain, the Chateau Queyras. The north fork is the Col d'Izoard. The right leads to St. Veran and Trip 19. The Col d'Izoard snakes up through very strange formations and barren gravel, an area called the Casse Deserte, to a summit with an obelisk monument, and winds down past a refuge with minimal facilities dating from Napoleon III, coming down right into **Briancon,** a pretty good sized city with another fortress.

Loop through the city to get on the main road and take the road east to Italy and the **Col de Montgenevre,** only fifteen kilometers up.

Then, six kilometers down into Italy, the road splits. A south leg climbs to a ski resort, really a pass, called **Sestriere,** then goes down toward Torino, passing **Fenestrelle** where there's a tempting climb north on a partly paved pass road, the **Col de Finestre,** which comes down near **Susa.**

The north leg goes directly to Susa (passing a toll tunnel at Bardonecchia that goes back into France). At Susa, a pass road climbs back north into France, passing along a lake, over the Col du Mt. Cenis and down into the Val d'Arc, just below the Col de l'Iseran (Trip 17).

Head downstream, west, in the Val d'Arc as far as St. Michel de Maurienne, where one of the wildest passes of the

Alps climbs right up south, the **Col du Galibier.** Before tackling the wonderful high stuff, the road climbs the **Col du Telegraphe,** then begins the real climb over Galibier. Coming down the south side of the Col, there are views of the junction below with the top of the **Col du Lautaret,** which is an east-west road.

From the junction, it's an easy ride on down to Briancon and Guillestre.

Trip 19   Col Agnel and Col di Sampeyre

Distance	*230 kilometers*
Terrain	*Little roads over high passes*
Highlights	*Four high passes, two unknown, seldom traveled ★ ★Col Agnel (dell'Agnello, in Italian) (2744 meters), ★ ★Col di Sampeyre (2284 meters), Col de Larche (Maddelena in Italian) (1996 meters), Col de Vars (2111 meters), Col de Lombarde (2351 meters)*

Head out of Guillestre on the Col d'Izoard road to Chateau Queyras and on toward St. Veran. (There's a dead-end road that climbs up behind the Chateau fortress to 2257 meters.) Before St. Veran, turn through the village Molines, which doesn't believe in street repair. Not to worry. Above the village is smooth narrow asphalt, climbing very high in a broad valley above the tree line to the Col Agnel and the Italian border. This little road is one of the highest in the Alps, and seldom rates a border guard. Sometimes, back at Molines there's a "ferme," closed, sign. But the road is opened for the

The Col d'Izoard, between Briancon and Guillestre, is full of strange formations. Napoleon slept here.

Giro d'Italia bicycle race very early in June. So go for it. Down below the pass, in Italy, there may be a bar across the road, but just join the locals driving around it.

Down about thirty-five kilometers into Italy at a village called **Sampeyre,** there's a pass of the same name, **Col di Sampeyre,** even less traveled, heading up and south. There's an interesting metal sculpture at the top. Then down the south side at the village, **Elva,** there's a little church with a very fine Renaissance fresco. What's it doing here? The ristorante in Elva will lend you a key to the church while it prepares your very Italian lunch. The descent south from Elva is spectacular. And the artist must have come through this gorge 400 years ago.

Back on the valley road, below Elva and the gorge, head downstream to **Donero,** a town about out of the mountains with tree shaded streets. Then south toward **Cuneo,** and back to France on the **Col de Maddalena** road. It's a more major crossing, signed for **Argentera,** a village near the border. Two full lanes with a few sweepers. At the top, it's **Col de Larche.** There are a couple of good bends on the way down to the valley road which it joins just south of the Col de Vars and north of **Jausiers.** Head back over the Col de Vars for Guillestre and St. Veran. (Roads south are in the next trip, Trip 20.)

Or, instead of crossing back into France on the main Col de Maddalena road, connecting to the Col de Vars, it's possible to cross the border on a seldom traveled high pass, the **Col de Lombarde,** which ties in with the south end of the passes in Trip 20. West from Cuneo toward the French border on the Col de Maddalena road, after the village of **Vinadio,** the narrow Col de Lombarde heads south. It is a lot of fun on the Italian climb to the summit. (At about 2,000 meters elevation, the road straight ahead dead ends. The pass road cuts back to the left.) A few kilometers down into France, the road enters a ski resort called **Isola 2000,** apparently the elevation. On into **Isola,** in the valley below, the road is aligned to get busloads of skiers up to Isola 2000. The lower Isola is on the south end of the **Col du Restefond,** which leads north to the Col de Vars.

Trip 20   The Really High Stuff

Distance   *About 280 kilometers*

Terrain   *High rugged mountains and roads*

Highlights   *Exotic wild scenery, Col de Vars (2111 meters), ★Col du Restefond (2678 meters), ★ ★la Bonette (2862 meters), Col de Roubion (1678 meters), Col Valberg (1668 meters), ★Col de la Cayolle (2327 meters), ★Col d'Allos (2240 meters)*

Climb southeasterly from Guillestre over the Col de Vars, to Jausiers where the Col du Restefond road heads for Nice and the Riviera. The road squiggles up quickly to the pass which may not be open until mid-summer. It is not a commercial route. Near the top of the col there's a loop road called **la Bonette** which might be the highest paved road in the Alps. It climbs up around a peak to a high point where many seem to have been unable to restrain themselves from leaving a mark of their visit. Near the loop junction are two arrow signs. One pointing north reads "Paris." One pointing south reads "Nice."

From the col it's about 50 kilometers south to the first intersection at **St. Sauveur.** Instead of going on to Nice, turn west over two low passes, the **Col de Roubion** and the **Valberg.** At Valberg there's the **Hotel Le Chalet Suisse** that advertises itself as having winter sports only 80 kilometers from Nice. F-06470 Valberg; phone: 049 302-5009; fax: 049 302-6192.

West of Valberg, at **Guillaumes,** is the **Col de la Cayolle** road, heading north to **Barcelonnette** and Guillestre.

The **Col d'Allos** roughly parallels the Col de la Coyolle to the west. It wanders a bit farther getting to Barcelonnette and is even less developed.

There are endless twisty roads and colorful gorges farther south, leading to the Mediterranean, but that will have to be another book.

The Col de la Cayolle is just a few kilometers north and a couple thousand meters up from Nice and Monte Carlo on the sunny Mediterranean. The road was part of Napolean's route from Elba.

South of
Andermatt

Lago Maggiore

If it gets a bit chilly or misty up in the high county, just do what the Swiss do: head for **Lugano** or **Locarno,** down in that Italian-speaking, pasta-eating part of Switzerland called Ticino. It's only an hour or two away. Hawaii, it's not. But around the lake shores there are real, if dwarf, palm trees, and oleander and hibiscus blooms—probably in pots—even while the snowy mountain peaks are still in sight. And there are some pretty good roads to get there on.

Locarno is on the north shore of a long, large lake called Maggiore. Part of the lake is in Italy, the rest in Switzerland. Lugano is on a smaller lake called Lugano, a bit southeast of Locarno. Why must the names sound so much alike? To confuse us.

Locarno, on **Lago Maggiore,** is small, sunny, and closer to the mountains than Lugano. It has hotels on the lake, on the hills, and in neighboring villages.

Right on the lake in Locarno is the **Beau-Rivage.** Rooms with a view of the lake are a bit more than "garden views;" Viale Verbano 31, or Box 43; CH-6600 Locarno-Muralto; phone: 091 743-1355; fax: 091 743-9409. Just a few blocks uphill and down in price is a plain, practical hotel, **Hotel Carmine;** Via Sempione 10; phone: 091 743-6033; fax: 091 743-8433. Across Lago Maggiore from Locarno, about 20 kilometers around the north tip of the lake, is **San Nazzaro,** where a modest hotel squeezed on the water's edge has great views across to Locarno and the Alps beyond from the dining room and some of the guest rooms; **Albergo Consolina;** CH-6575 San Nazzaro; phone: 091 794-2335 (the back rooms are close to a train track).

From Lugano, the southernmost Swiss city, almost surrounded by Italy, the border crossing in the direction of Lago Maggiore is signed "Ponte Tresa." At Ponte Tresa there's a pleasant waterfront hotel restaurant called del Pesce.

From the high Alps there are three pass roads leading down to Lago Maggiore: from Andermatt, the St. Gotthard Pass; from the Rhone Valley, the Simplon Pass; and from **Graubunden** and the Rhine Valley, the **Passo del San Bernardino.**

Trip 21 Passo San Gottardo

Distance	*About 100 kilometers from Andermatt to Locarno, one way*
Terrain	*Modern pass road and valley autostrada*
Highlights	*Quick way to get down out of the mountains, Passo San Gottardo (2108 meters)*

The St. Gotthard Pass from Andermatt (in Ticino, it's Passo San Gottardo) leads right down to Locarno. It's described in Trip 2, out of Andermatt. Once off the pass, it's autostrada all the way.

Trip 22   Passo del San Bernardino

Distance   *About 105 kilometers from Chur, in the Rhine Valley, to Locarno, one way*

Terrain   *Tight, twisting, narrow mountain pass road, followed by high speed swooping across huge bridges to autostrada*

Highlights   *Rustic cafe on top of pass, exhilarating swoops, Passo del San Bernardino (2065 meters)*

From the Rhein (we spell it Rhine) valley in Graubunden, the San Bernardino Pass (in Ticino, Passo del San Bernardino) makes a direct and good ride connection to Locarno. The pass road is a sweeping, high-speed, two-lane Autobahn most of the way from Chur in Graubunden in the Rhine Valley to Locarno. Most of the way it's possible to dodge back and forth keeping to pieces of non-Autobahn roads. There's an all-weather tunnel under the highest peaks, but there's a twisty, attention-demanding road up over the pass, above the tunnel, that's a motorcycle delight. A restaurant on a lake at the top makes a great stop, and a regular *Tofftreffpunkt.* Dine rustically upstairs if it's not comfortable sitting out.

The south side of the San Bernardino is on a magnificent series of sweepers with high arched bridges carrying the road back and forth over the valley below. In the lower valley is the village of Grono where Kiwi helmets are made.

Near **Bellinzona** the San Bernardino road joins the San Gottardo autostrada.

Trip 23   Simplon Pass

Distance *About 100 kilometers from Brig in the Rhone Valley to Locarno, one way*

Terrain *High pass with high speed sweepers in (CH); Val Cannobina in Italy is narrow and tight*

Highlights *Narrow and tight and fun, used by locals only, leads to lakefront road; Simplon Pass (2006 meters), a major pass between Italy and Switzerland; charming Centovalli and Val Cannobina, Swiss Army may be on maneuvers*

From the Rhone Valley, the Simplon Pass (Sempione in Italian) is in Switzerland all the way across, then enters Italy at its southern base. From here, there are a couple of fun connections back to Switzerland and Locarno: the **Centovalli** and **Val Cannobina.** Just after entering Italy at the base of the Sempione, before the Italian industrial town of **Domodossola,** the Centovalli road heads up and east toward **Malesco.** From Malesco, the road heads into Switzerland and down to Locarno. A pleasant route.

For a more challenging ride, head up and around Malesco's village church (not the big domed basilica on the edge of town which, incidentally, has a gruesome collection of pictures of vehicle accidents) and up over a narrow pass, the Valle Cannobina road. Near a tunnel at the top, right on the edge of a lush, green, peaceful gorge, are some small memorial markers commemorating Italian partisans killed by the retreating Germans at the end of World War II. The road works down in a one-lane-wide collection of twisties through green forest to Lago Maggiore at an Italian town called **Cannobio.** From Cannobio it's a short ride north along the lakeshore to Switzerland and Locarno. (Lakeshore traffic can be tedious, and this little jaunt, however nice the views, may be all that's needed to illustrate the point.) Both the Centovalli and the Val Cannobina roads have rustic places to stop for refreshment.

Trip 24 Valle Maggia

• •

Distance   *Valle Maggia, about 120 kilometers round trip from Locarno*

Terrain   *Small, twisty roads into remote, high villages surrounded by giant mountains*

Highlights   *To explore where no one goes, try these dead-end valleys*

A couple of kilometers out the Centovalli road from Locarno, it splits. The **Valle Maggia** road goes north and climbs through quiet villages with stone houses and roofs of huge stone slabs. The road narrows to work up switchbacks to high Alpine lakes where it dead-ends, 50 kilometers from town. Nobody there.

Over toward the base of Passo Sempione, on the Italian side of the border above Domodossola, the **Val d'Ossola** climbs north almost to the Nufenen Pass in Switzerland. There's a *rifugio* near the lake at its top. (*Rifugios* are Italian institutions, usually staffed by a resident family to serve Alpine travelers and workers.)

South of Domodossola, at Villadossola, a wild little road climbs the **Val di Antrona**. There's a rifugio there, too.

Trip 25   Highs Over Lago Maggiore

Distance	*220 kilometers*
Terrain	*little mountain roads right behind the lake congestion*
Highlights	*A pass no tourist sees, Passo Alpi di Neggia (1395 meters), ferry across the lake (toll), Mattarone (1491 meters)*

On the east shore of the lake, south of Locarno, still in Switzerland, at **Vira,** take the steep little road uphill signed Indemini. That's a town at the Swiss-Italian border. Getting there, it quickly leaves houses behind and winds up and over the **Passo Alpi di Neggia.** Border guards will be surprised to see you. You may be their only customers for the day. In Italy, ride down to the lake at Maccagno and south along the lake shore to **Laveno,** where there's a ferry across the lake to **Intra** on the west shore. There are a couple of ferries an hour, and the ride takes about twenty minutes.

Follow the west lake shore south to **Stresa,** a fairly congested tourist town. Once there, head inland on cobbled streets, west for **Mattarone.** It's signed. You're quickly in the woods. At the top there's a cable car and a restaurant. There's also a toll. Head down west to the next lake, **Lago d'Orta,** and then north to **Omegna.** Might as well take the autostrada from **Gravellona** to Piedimulera where there's a dead-end road up the Val Anzasca to a ski resort, **Macugnaga,** separated by Monte Rosa from Zermatt, Switzerland.

Back in the valley, take the **Malesco** road from Domodossola to Switzerland.

East of
Andermatt

▲ St. Moritz

East of Andermatt, over the Oberalp Pass, is the biggest and wildest of Swiss cantons, Graubunden, home of world-famous winter sports, **St. Moritz, Davos,** and more. Part of Graubunden is in the Rhein Tal (Rhein Valley) draining toward the North Sea, and part of it is in the Inn Tal, usually called Engadin, running toward Innsbruck, the Danube, and the Black Sea. A few parts in the south run into Italy and the Adriatic. Getting back and forth between these valleys across great mountain ranges makes for some good roads and good riding.

St. Moritz, in the high Engadin (valley of the Inn), is higher than a lot of passes, at 1822 meters. Even though it's high and cool and famous, St. Moritz and its neighboring resort villages are a logical base for exploring the great roads of Graubunden. Most facilities are available. Its reputation as the old-time playground of royalty means that there are old-time posh establishments, but there are plenty of places for ordinary bike riders. St. Moritz-Dorf (the German word for "village" is *Dorf*) is on the north slopes of the Engadin, up the mountainside from St. Moritz on the main valley road.

Right in the center of the Dorf, facing one of the few outdoor eating plazas (actually, one of the few level places in St. Moritz), is the **Hauser Hotel;** CH-7500 St. Moritz-Dorf; phone: 081 833-4402; fax: 081 833-1029. Right behind the Hauser is the **Hotel Crystal;** CH-7500 St. Moritz-Dorf; phone: 081 832-1165; fax: 081 833-6445. Both are modern and touristy, but right in the middle of the village.

Traffic through and near St. Moritz is encouraged to use the main valley road below the Dorf, but there is a good high road running east and west from the plaza at the Hauser Hotel.

For a real experience in how a Swiss hotel can coddle, and at about the cost of a modest hotel in the city, treat yourself to Hotel Le Prese in the village of **Le Prese,** south of St.

Moritz, on the other side of the **Bernina Pass,** and almost completely surrounded by Italy. In an old building that has been modernized, the Hotel Le Prese is guaranteed to make everyone feel luxuriously cared for. There's a large outdoor pool. Almost all guests are annual regulars, with hardly a foreigner (non-Swiss) among them. Since there's a dress code, the management may discreetly arrange a dinner table with heavy linen and silver in the handsome bar room. **Hotel Le Prese;** CH-7749 Le Prese; phone: 081 844-0333; fax: 081 844-0835.

Escape St. Moritz, down the Engadin (northeast) about twelve kilometers to **Zuoz,** a small village with cobblestone streets and beautiful quaint houses, some several hundred years old, with shops and banks and cows. The main valley road bypasses the town on the south bank of the Inn River, leaving Zuoz high—1716 meters—on the north. In Zuoz is the **Post Hotel Engiadina,** complete with an outdoor pool for the brave. CH-7524 Zuoz; phone: 081 854-1021; fax: 081 854-3303.

Upstream (southwest) from St. Moritz, toward the **Maloja Pass** is a village **Sils-Baselgia,** with Hotel Margna. There are two entrances to the village from the main valley road, and the hotel's at the upstream one, closer to the pass. There's an adjacent "garni," lower priced. **Hotel Margna;** CH-7515 Sils-Baselgia; phone: 081 826-5307; fax: 081 826-5470. The owner is a U.S. Navy veteran.

Trip 26 Vorderrhein (the 'Front Rhine')

. . . .

Distance *About 150 kilometers from Andermatt to St. Moritz, one way*
Terrain *Narrow cliff-hanging road to major mountain highway*
Highlights *Brief glimpse at a Switzerland no tourist sees*

The summit of the Oberalp Pass is just a few sweeping kilometers up from Andermatt. Then there's a pretty quick and tight descent as far as Disentis, followed by a long ride down the Vorderrhein valley (the "front Rhine") toward Chur, the capital of Graubunden, and the next good roads. Along the way, the Rhein goes through one of those *schluchts*. The highway has to go up and around to the north of the Schlucht through the ski resorts of Laax and Flims. But there's a neat alternative. Chiseled out of the cliffs on the south side is a tight, narrow, cliff-hanging road known only to locals and exploring motorcyclists. It's easy to catch at **Ilanz** by crossing into the village from the highway and heading east, downstream, at the village square. The east end of the road is at **Bonaduz,** on the main routes to St. Moritz. From Bonaduz, the main road goes to **Tiefencastel** and then over the **Julier Pass.** (For more information about these roads, see Trip 27.)

To extend the exploring, there's more high road paralleling the main one. Turn south off the main valley road about twenty kilometers upstream (west) of Ilanz. (At the time of the turnoff, the main road is briefly on the south bank of the Rhein.) It's marked "**Obersaxon,**" which is a region, not a town. The road climbs through high meadows with views over the whole valley, then comes down to the main square in Ilanz.

Trip 27 Hinterrhein (the 'Back Rhine')

· ·

Distance *About 170 kilometers from St. Moritz, plus 50 to Juf*

Terrain *Narrow, tight, steep climb, hairpins, and tunnels on Splugen; challenging, modern mountain highway on Maloja and Julier*

Highlights *Audacious mountain road, awesome gorges, rustic rifugio, highest village in Switzerland, Maloja Pass (1815 meters), ★ ★ Splugen Pass (2113 meters), Juf and the Via Mala, ★ Julier Pass (2284 meters)*

Heading upstream (southwest) through the Engadin valley from St. Moritz, past some nice lakes, you don't feel like you're climbing. Then, suddenly, you come upon a real switchback downhill, the Maloja Pass. You're already at the top. The Maloja heads down through some pleasant Swiss villages, one of which has such a narrow street that there's a traffic signal at each end to let vehicles pass one way at a time. The road heads over the Italian border. A bit into Italy, in the larger town of **Chiavenna,** there's a little traffic circle (watch for the brown sign, *Passo Spluga*) and the beginning of a wild climb up the **Splugen Pass** back toward Switzerland. (For roads south of Chiavenna, see Trip 37.)

The pass road often just barely hangs on a cliff, often hairpins in a tunnel, often works through stone snow shed tunnels that seem hardly helmet high and must have been built a century ago. Yet after snaking through stacks of cliff-hanging hairpins and one-way tunnels, in typical Italian fashion, the road ends in villages with people and trucks and buses, all using the road as their only connection to the world.

Short of the top of the pass, just below the face of a Mussolini-massive stone dam, is a typical Italian mountain rifugio, called Rifugio Stuetta, a fun place for a lunch, cappuccino, or good Italian hot chocolate. In a rustic wood-paneled room with a tiny bar, the host family will see that some kind of food, usually pasta and salad just waiting to be made, is available to refresh a weary traveler. It's a good place to remember that *bolognese* is meat sauce and *pomodoro* is tomato sauce, that oil and vinegar is the salad dressing of

Italy, and that *formaggio,* cheese, will probably be Parmesan. Almost all remote Italian passes have these inns, staffed by a family in residence, which provide shelter and food to road workers and travelers. Invariably, there's one clean, though small, toilet.

Higher, just a few switchbacks below the summit, is a village, Monte Spluga, 1908 meters, with a small hotel only 150 years old. **Hotel Vittoria;** Via Dogana 12; I-23020 Monte Spluga; phone: 03 435-4250; fax: 03 433-6197. Rustic.

Back in Switzerland, the road pulls one of the most amazing and oft-photographed series of ladder switchbacks in the Alps. The road goes back and forth so often on the alluvial mountain slope that you can pass by the same vehicles going in the same direction time after time.

Ten kilometers over the border into Switzerland, the pass road meets the high-speed San Bernardino Autobahn, a two-lane freeway. This is the valley of the Hinterrhein, the "back Rhine," to go with the Vorderrhein, the "front Rhine" leading down from the Oberalp.

Just ten kilometers down the Autobahn from the Splugen, an Autobahn Ausfahrt (exit) called **Avers-Rofla** leads to an adjoining Schlucht, and a Tofftreffpunkt at Gasthof Roflaschlucht. Opposite, a winding and deserted road leads south up to **Juf,** the highest permanent town in Switzerland, at 2126 meters. You'll find no tourists on this road.

Farther down the Autobahn, just before the Vorderrhein and Hinterrhein meet, is the **Via Mala,** the "bad way." The Autobahn sweeps through the gorge of the Via Mala in tunnels and bridges that make it easy to miss the narrow, deep gorge that for centuries was the "bad way." Take the Via Mala Ausfahrt and look down on what a frightening journey it must have been.

Below the Via Mala at **Thusis,** take the road toward Tiefencastel and the Julier Pass. The first part is another engineering tour de force, sweeping through an impossible gorge, playing back and forth at times with the Glacier Express train. Tiefencastel, wedged into a tiny valley, has gas, hotels, and a church typical of Romansch style: square stucco bell tower with an octagonal belfry topped by a dome.

The Julier road starts in Tiefencastel and climbs long, snaking up a gorge, then by a lake. Facilities at the top are good only for a postcard. Because the Engadin around St. Moritz is so high it's not far down to them from the top of the Julier into Silvaplana, a town with cute hotels and restaurants, and on into St. Moritz.

Almost all remote Italian passes have a rifugio staffed by a family in residence. This one, just shy of the Splugen Pass summit on the Italian side, is the Rifugio Stuetta. A welcome sight for the weary biker.

The north slope of Splugen Pass has an amazing series of switchbacks. This is September with a light covering of new snow that has been plowed. A few kilometers on, there's no snow.

Trip 28   Albula Pass Connections

Distance	*About 190 kilometers from St. Moritz*
Terrain	*Four high passes and one medium high pass*
Highlights	*Cute Romansch villages, views of Glacier Express trestles, ski resorts, ★ ★ Moonscape on Albula Pass (2312 meters), Lenzerheide (1547 meters), Wolfgang Pass (1631 meters), ★ Fluela Pass (2383 meters), Arosa (1775 meters)*

Right in the middle of a little village called **La Punt,** 12 kilometers down the Engadin (north) from St. Moritz, is the **Albula Pass** turnoff. It looks like a street of no significance between two buildings. The Albula is a back road. It climbs quickly above the tree line to the summit, and then bobs and weaves across a wild, rocky no-man's-land before starting down through lovely remote Romansch villages to Tiefencastel.

While the Julier Pass is considered the main auto road into St. Moritz, the train takes the Albula. Several of the bridges used by the Glacier Express along the route are famous on postcards and travelogues. Around the town of Bergun, the train makes several climbing loops inside the mountain, and below Filisur, the train crosses a gorge on a high stone arch viaduct, only to disappear at a right angle into the sheer granite cliff face.

The Albula leads down to Tiefencastel, quite a crossroads in its narrow gorge. This is where the Julier and Thusis roads meet the Albula Pass, plus a shortcut road toward **Davos** where the **Fluela Pass** starts, and the **Lenzerheide** road north over Lenzerheide. (For some reason Lenzerheide is never called a "pass," even though it's always listed as one.)

Lenzerheide is where the book *Heidi* is supposed to take place. It is very pretty country, but not exotic. The area centers around Chur, the canton capital, a large city with motorcycle shops and services, but the Lenzerheide road stays on the hillside above Chur and connects directly to the San Bernardino Autobahn.

East above Chur is **Arosa,** a well-known ski resort, accessible only by a very twisty road that follows the arc of a mountain stream called Plessur for thirty kilometers. Arosa, at 1775 meters, is the end of the road. It's necessary to go into Chur to catch the Arosa road.

A 15-kilometer jaunt north on the Autobahn brings the rider to **Landquart** and the **Wolfgang Pass** road to Davos. Just short of the summit of the Wolfgang Pass is Klosters, where some members of the British royal family have been known to ski.

A couple of kilometers over the Wolfgang is Davos, with a one-way loop street that makes for an easy return to the Fluela Pass road. The Fluela, which has a pleasant, rustic restaurant at the top, crosses back to the Engadin below St. Moritz.

Once, 500 motorcyclists, on a rally sponsored by Michael Krauser, paraded through Davos past a reviewing stand with some notables, while the Davos town band played and replayed Queen Liliuokalani's "Aloha Oe," "Farewell to Hawaii."

Trip 29 Italian Connections

Distance *About 230 kilometers*

Terrain *Endless tight hairpins on Stelvio, one of the highest passes in the Alps; short unpaved section on Umbrail Pass; challenging modern pass road on Bernina Pass*

Highlights *Good sweepers over ★ Bernina Pass (2328 meters) into Switzerland's farthest corner; a major motorcycle goal, the ★ ★ Passo dello Stelvio) (2758 meters), with restaurant terraces, and hotels, vendors on top; Swiss national park, Umbrail Pass (2501 meters), Ofen Pass (2149 meters)*

★

The Bernina Pass, south from St. Moritz, swoops down and around, bypassing Pontresina, a popular resort. Then after climbing the first switchbacks, and just over some railroad tracks, there's a view point with the best views of Piz Bernina (the highest peak of the area) and its glaciers. The restaurants at the top are serviceable. Just across the top is an intersection with a border crossing into the isolated Italian valley of **Livigno** (see Trip 30).

The sweeping southerly descent of the Bernina stays on good Swiss pavement. Below the town of Poschiavo is the little village of Le Prese, notable to bikers because of the train tracks that go down the middle of the street—well, almost the middle. It would be easier if they stayed in the middle. At the downhill end of the village, just as the tracks pull off to the side, is the Le Prese Hotel. Stop for lunch or refreshment on the lakefront terrace.

Recently an avalanche took out the road around the lake, below the hotel. Travelers had to take a boat across the lake until a precarious wooden ramp could be built. The ramp served until the permanent road could be rebuilt.

The Italian border is just a few kilometers on, with a steady parade of Italian cars crossing into Switzerland, tanking up on less expensive Swiss gas, and making a U-turn back to Italy. Not a bad idea.

Just into Italy is the Italian town of **Tirano,** where a turn north by the big yellow church starts the climb to the most famous motorcycle destination in the Alps, the **Passo dello Stelvio,** known in German as the Stilfser Joch (say "yoke".) At 2758 meters, it's one of the highest pass roads in the Alps. Every motorcyclist has to climb it. The collection of stalls, shops, restaurants, hotels, and even a bank at the top of the Stelvio probably does violate environmental sense, but the convenience is unmatched.

Italy is building a two-lane freeway up the lower part of the valley from Tirano as far as Bormio, but the road over the pass above Bormio can only be described as *laissez faire* Italian determination. It seems like half the hairpins in the Alps are on the Stelvio, 40 or so on each side. And they are hairpins, with practically zero inside radius. Where there's room, the road may be almost two lanes wide, but much of the time, one narrow lane seems to strain the limits of the slope. In some places, the hand-laid rock retaining walls have obviously been pushed beyond their limits, and the road has slipped a bit down the mountainside. The Italian solution is to bridge the gap by pouring asphalt in the crack.

The Stelvio clearly illustrates the problem of mountain road building and maintenance. Surrounded by high cliffs, the alluvial slope is the only possible place to hang a road. And the alluvial slope is inherently unstable. The alternative, often used elsewhere in Italy, is a tunnel deep inside the mountain. But that surely spoils the view.

There's a road sign repeatedly seen in Italy: *lavoro in corso*, "work in progress." It perhaps should read "work needs to be in progress."

Whether it's sunny or foggy or snowy or rainy, there are always bikes on Stelvio. It's a must-stop for lunch or cappuccino or just tire-kicking. The postcard vendors know their market: there are plenty of cards showing the road, some with bikes in the hairpins. Skiers are permitted and there's summer skiing on the glaciers. There are even a couple of hotels on the top. **Hotel Stilfser Joch** (also known as Passo dello Stelvio Hotel); fax: 034 290-3664. **Stelvio Hotel Perego** (recently remodeled); phone and fax: 034 290-4553.

The northeast side of the Stelvio is equally exciting. It is often marked *chiuso*, "closed," but traffic is usually going around the barricade.

Just short of the top of the Stelvio, on the southwest (Bormio) side, is a border crossing back into Switzerland. This is the **Umbrail Pass.** From the border crossing it's all downhill. A reasonable portion of it is not paved, but is maintained in good condition. It goes down to the main Swiss road in the handsome Romansch village of **Santa Maria,** where the **Ofen Pass** climbs back toward the Engadin.

A fascinating alternate route to Santa Maria is to continue on across the Stelvio and, at the Italian base town of **Prato,** head north on a beautiful side road past the **Castle of Lichtenburg** to **Glorenza** (Glurns in German). From Glorenza, it's 20 kilometers to the Swiss border and the Ofen Pass road.

Just north of Glorenza (in Italy) there's a wonderful hotel in the village of **Mals.** (It's actually on the Reschen Pass road.) With spacious rooms, views of the valley and mountains from every one, including the indoor pool, is **Hotel Garberhof;** I-39024 Mals; phone: 473 831399; fax: 473 831950. It's a good base for exploring the Passo dello Stelvio.

The last kilome-
ters near the top
of the Passo
dello Stelvio in
Italy hang pre-
cariously on an
alluvial slope.
On the east side,
the road has
been outlined by
an overnight
snowfall.

From a small
border station on
the Bernina Pass
in Switzerland, a
good Italian road
leads into duty-
free Livigno, an
Italian valley al-
most surrounded
by Switzerland,
where every-
thing, including
gasoline, is
tax-free.

There's always a
crowd on the top
of Passo dello
Stelvio. It isn't
pretty, but it's
exciting—sort of
a motorcycle
Mecca. There's
skiing all summer
on nearby gla-
ciers so there are
hotels and even a
bank on the pass.

Just inside the Swiss border, above Glorenza, is the Swiss village of **Mustair**. Right on the road is a small church dating from the time of Charlemagne, famous for the earliest frescoes in Europe. Most of the frescoes tell the story of John the Baptist. The main ones focus on the gruesome aspects: tied up before Solome, then his head on the platter, etc., in the almost comic-book art style of the Middle Ages. The parking lot is across from the church, but bikes can usually park on the sidewalk by the gate.

Santa Maria has a good hotel just above where the Umbrail Pass comes down into town. It has good parking, WCs, an outdoor terrace, and goulash soup. **Hotel Stelvio;** CH-7536 Santa Maria; phone: 081 858-5358; fax: 081 858-5039.

The Ofen Pass, heading back toward the Engadin and St. Moritz, passes through the Swiss National Park. The park area seems very arid by Alpine standards, looking much like western parks in the U.S. From the Ofen Pass road, there's a one-way-at-a-time toll tunnel back into Italy and the Livigno valley (Trip 30). The small, narrow tunnel is several kilometers long. Traffic signals control the direction of traffic flow.

Trip 30 Duty-Free Livigno & Passo di Gavia

Distance	*About 230 kilometers*
Terrain	*Rugged, high, challenging mountain roads*
Highlights	*Forcola di Livigno (2315 meters), Passo d'Eira (2210 meters), Passo di Foscagno (2291 meters), Passo dell'Aprica (1176 meters), a high valley of Italy where everything is tax-free, including gasoline; also one of the Alps' more famous challenges, the ★ ★ Passo di Gavia (2621 meters), ★Passo di Mortirolo (1896 meters), unknown to most map makers*

Just over the Bernina Pass from St. Moritz is a border station, open during the day, into Italy. It opens to a nicely paved Italian Alpine pass road, Forcola di Livigno, that descends to an Alpine curiosity, the duty-free high Alpine valley of Livigno. The valley is pretty well surrounded by Switzerland. The only Italian road out is up over two passes. Everything in Livigno is tax-free, including gas.

Free enterprise has not treated Livigno with gentleness. It's a hodgepodge. Most of what merchants think visitors should buy won't fit too well on a bike. Hotels and restaurants are adequate, but nothing special.

Besides the road from the Bernina Pass, there are two other ways out of Livigno. Straight down the valley, through the town and out the other side, a road winds around a lake to the toll tunnel back into the Swiss National Park. It's a one-way-at-a-time tunnel, controlled by lights (Trip 29).

The other way is through Italy, a bumpy 50-kilometer trip over two passes, the **Passo d'Eira** and the **Passo di Foscagno,** that few tourists or visiting motorcyclists see. These pass roads lead to Bormio, the base of the Passo dello Stelvio and also the take-off point for Passo di Gavia, one of the higher roads in the Alps. Follow the brown signs for the Gavia in downtown Bormio.

From Bormio, the first 15 kilometers of the Gavia are standard highway. Then the fun begins. Much of the descent on the south side of the Gavia is narrow and unpaved, hanging on little ledges with rocky hairpins supported by flimsy old rock walls with hardly a piece of string or a tree branch for a guard rail.

This is another of those roads where "chiuso" (closed) probably means "travel at your own risk." Even when the road is closed, the rifugio at the top may be open, but there are no other services on the 35-kilometer crossing to **Ponte di Legno.**

Ponte di Legno is on a main east-west highway. Head west in the direction of **Edolo.** (Edolo is a few kilometers north of Trip 37.)

About five kilometers before (east of) Edolo is the turn for a fantastic little road used on the Giro d'Italia bicycle race, but otherwise forgotten, **Passo di Mortirolo.** No maps show this road correctly. It is paved but narrow, and goes across the mountain between the villages of **Monno** and **Mazzo.** In Mazzo, its north end, it's signed "Passo di Mortirolo." At the other end, near Edolo, the only sign is "Manno." At the top, a small road leads west, while the pass road zigzags down, one lane of narrow pavement covered with painted slogans for the bicycle racers. Mazzo at the north end is in the Adda valley. Downstream, west, is Tirano and the entrance to the Bernina Pass. Upstream, east, is the Passo dello Stelvio.

Should you choose to continue on through Edolo, instead of Passo di Mortirolo, the **Passo dell'Aprica** is straight ahead. The Aprica isn't high but has some ski hotels and restaurants right on the road through town. The west side of the Aprica has sweeping views of the Adda Valley which leads toward Lake Como. But before that, about seven kilometers below Aprica, just after a tight curve that reverses the traverse, a little sign saying *Stazzona* points at a little road into the woods that works down the mountain to the main road toward Tirano.

At Tirano, the big yellow church marks the gateway back to Switzerland, Le Prese, the Bernina Pass, and St. Moritz.

Sud Tirol

Handsome is the word to describe **Merano,** Alto Adige, also known as Meran, Sud Tirol. Giant trees shade its streets. A mountain torrent, the Passiria in Italian, Passeier in German, regularly used for whitewater racing pours through its heart. Flowered promenades with coffee houses and *gelaterias* (ice cream parlors) follow the edge of the torrent. Its little medieval section has narrow arch-shaded streets lined with shops selling everything: bananas, nuts, pastries, leather goods, toys, the latest fashions. Behind the shops are beer gardens with the best Austrian and Italian food. Mountain peaks surround the town, lower slopes laden with apples and pears and vines. It's been the favorite spa of kaisers and kings. Yet Americans never stop in Merano. Say "Merano" to an American travel agent, and you will be corrected, "You mean Milano." No, Merano.

Merano is one of those places that has become Italian instead of Austrian only in the twentieth century. Much of the culture is both Austrian and Italian, and most everything has a name in both languages. You'll find pasta right beside Wienerschnitzel on many menus.

The mountainsides are lined with hotels. **Hotel Augusta** is a handsome yellow structure in a sort of Austrian Victorian style, secluded in a shaded garden just off the promenade. You'll find it at 2 Via Otto Huber; I-39012 Merano; Alto Adige; phone: 047 34-9570 (or Otto Huber Strasse 2; I-39012 Meran Sud Tirol); fax: 047 34-9750.

The giant old time hotel "spa" of Merano is the Kurhotel Palace. It looks like a palace, sitting well back from the street. It has huge halls and lots of gilt, only slightly faded. In low season prices are reasonable, especially for rooms facing the town. There's an outdoor-indoor pool with an electric eye to open the glass door between them as you swim up to it. Across the street is a shady park with a statue of the Empress Elizabeth, wife of Franz-Joseph. (Remember, she was assassinated in Geneve by a guy wielding scissors.) **Kurhotel Palace;** I-39012 Merano; phone: 047 321-1300; fax: 047 323-4181. Coat and tie required at dinner!

Up the Passeier twenty kilometers is **St. Leonhard** (San Leonardo, in Italian), a village with several good Tiroler style hotels, like **Hotel Stroblhof;** I-39015 St. Leonhard; phone: 047 365-6128; fax: 047 365-6468. It's right on the main street where all the bikes pass.

Thirteen kilometers west of Merano in the direction of Reschen Pass and Stelvio, just past the village of Naturns, a great road called Schnals Tal (Val Senales) climbs north toward the glaciers. The road's another alpine wonder. Several kilometers up the way, at **Karthaus** (Certosa), is **Hotel Schnals Tal;** No. 60; I-39020 Karthaus; phone: 047 39-8102. Farther up the valley, at the top of the road, a cable car takes skiers up to summer skiing on the **Similaun Glacier,** the glacier where the multi-thousand-year-old ice man was recently found.

Up the mountain east of Merano is **Hafling,** famous for the small horses called Haflingers. From Hafling, a small road hangs on the mountain all the way south to **Bolzano** (in Bolzano, follow signs to **Jenesian** to reach Hafling). (See Trip 34.)

Merano is a delight to be in, but it can be a pain to ride through. Brown signs do mark routes through town to the nearby passes.

Above the treeline on the Italian side of Timmels Joch, above St. Leonhard in the Sud Tirol, there are plenty of hairpins.

Trip 31 Timmels Joch

Distance *About 100 kilometers round trip to top of the pass*

Terrain *Some congestion near Merano, narrow twisting climb, dark tunnel, on Italian side; more moderate on Austrian side*

Highlights *Exhilarating views of glaciated peaks, connection to Austrian Tirol and Germany (toll), ★ ★ Timmels Joch (2509 meters)*

★ ★

The raging river through Merano is the Passer. Follow it upstream, north from Merano, 20 kilometers to St. Leonhard (San Leonardo in Italian), at the base of the **Timmels Joch.** On the way, the road passes the home of Andreas Hofer, a sort-of George Washington of the Sud Tirol (only he didn't win). The house is now a Gasthaus.

The Timmels Joch is the lower leg of the fork in the road at St. Leonhard. It's a secondary road, narrow, tight, and twisty, hanging over deep canyons with a horizon studded with snowy peaks, and with some dark, rough-bottomed tunnels at the top.

In St. Leonhard there's a little bridge across the river. You may take it and follow a mini-one-laner through the forests as far up as **Moos** where it rejoins the main Timmels Joch road.

Across the border at the top, on the Austrian side, there's a good restaurant. The road quality improves—as well it should, because Austria collects a toll. It leads in a few kilometers to ski areas at Hochgurgl, **Obergurgl,** and Unter-gurgl, then into a long, pleasant Austrian valley. (See Trip 48 for a hotel in Vent Tal, below the "gurgl's".)

Trip 32   Reschen Pass

Distance	*About 160 kilometers round trip to top of pass*
Terrain	*Gentle climb on Italian side, a little more precipitous on Austrian side*
Highlights	*Orchards and farms, toll-free connection to Germany, leads to Stelvio, Reschen Pass (Passo Resia) (1504 meters)*

The main highway skirts around Merano on the west, and climbs a long valley toward the low **Reschen Pass** into Austria. On the way, it passes the turnoff for Schnals Tal, the Stelvio Pass, and the turnoff for Santa Maria into Switzerland, and then some World War I forts and a ghost village sunk beneath the waters behind a dam with only the church steeple showing. Shaped like big igloos, the concrete forts were built by the Austrians to defend the pass from the Italians in World War I. Because the pass is low and has no toll, it's a favorite of Germans pulling trailers with low-powered sedans. It leads into the Engadin below St. Moritz and the Inn valley.

Trip 33 Merano

· ·

Distance   *About 170 kilometers*

Terrain   *Steep climbs and descents with hairpins, some narrow roads, over four high passes*

Highlights   *Neat farms, forests, prosperous villages, Tirolian culture, ★ Jaufen Pass (Passo di Monte Giovo) (2094 meters), ★ Penser Joch (Passo di Pennes) (2214 meters), Mendel Pass (Passo di Mendola) (1363 meters), Gampen Joch (Passo di Palade) (1518 meters)*

Starting at that fork in St. Leonhard, take the upper tine, the Jaufen Pass, a tight, narrow climb through forests, that bursts above the tree line. There are only sandwich shops on the top, and then a quick, steep descent into **Sterzing** (called Vipiteno in Italian). Sterzing is on the Brennero-Modena Autostrada, the major route between the cities of Italy and Germany.

Sterzing has an interesting but gotta-walk-in-to-see-it arcaded old street from the Middle Ages, similar to that in Merano, with many good restaurants. Try the four-cheese linguini. There's also a bike shop that deals in Moto Guzzi and choppers. On the wall is a photocopy of the cover of an American magazine featuring one of the local choppers.

The junction of the Jaufen Pass road with the **Penser Joch** road is before Sterzing, so it's not necessary to go into the town unless you want to check it out. The Penser Joch road is marked with one of those brown pass signs. It's a great twisting climb to the top, back up above the tree line, where there's a good rifugio restaurant. Then there's a long descent southerly, almost like a trip back in time, past flowering meadows and little villages and sturdy farmhouses. The valley, called Saren Tal (Val Sarentino in Italian), is completely Austrian in culture. Then some arched tunnels through a gorge and by a castle on a peak into Bolzano, a prosperous industrial city.

Bolzano (Bozen in German) is at the bottom of the deep canyon used by the Brennero-Modena Autostrada. It's just a couple of hours north to Munchen, and less than that south to Venezia. Bolzano has good motorcycle shops.

Keeping to the west through Bolzano, follow brown signs to **Passo di Mendola** (Mendel Pass), and regular signs to Eppan and Kaltern, towns on the way.

Mendel Pass climbs along cliffs with views of the deep canyon, the autostrada and railroad in it, and the river that made it, the Adige. Then it climbs into park-like green forests. A good picnic area. The culture is very Austrian.

Just over the pass where it's Italian again, turn toward **Fondo,** and from there onto the **Gampen Joch** road. The Gampen Joch (Passo di Palade in Italian) climbs up, over, and down, with arched stone barriers on the edge of the pavement, typical of the Austrian Empire days. Toward Merano is the suburb **Marling** (Marlengo in Italian), with a good BMW dealer, well appreciated for having pick-your-own cherries, with one-pole ladders at the ready. Like many European BMW dealers, this one handles both cars and bikes.

Trip 34   One Lane Roads Across Sud Tirol

• •

Distance   *About 240 kilometers*

Terrain   *A couple of high passes, more modest heights, attention demanding narrow paved roads and the wonderful and handsome farming culture of the Sud Tirol. Weaving one lane mountain roads, some of them found in Trips 27, 29, 37, and 38, starting from the Austrian Ost (east) Tirol near Lienz, across Italian Sud Tirol to the Austrian Tirol near Imst. (Because the culture is Austrian, the German names for places are used here, even though the country is Italy. Where Italian names might be helpful, they're mentioned.)*

Highlights   *Green forests, very neat farms with sturdy barns, and quaint villages all in park-like settings. Nothing flat. No busses. Plenty of facilities*

★ ★

Take this route and discover the magic of the Sud Tiroler culture. For centuries the area was Austrian. At Versailles after World War I, it became Italian. Now, everything has an Italian name and the best map is the Italian Touring Club (T.C.I.) one called Trentino/Alto Adige. On the ground, everything is very Austrian. Village churches have Austrian steeples, not Italian campaniles, restaurants have

Wienerschnitzel rather than pasta. The flag of Sud Tirol is red and white, remarkably similar to the Austrian flag. It is flown proudly from house, barn, and church tower on special days. The route description here is from east to west.

Start at the east end of the route, where the Sud Tirol meets the Ost Tirol, which happens to be the Austrian/Italian border, atop the **Staller Sattel** (NW of Lienz). It's one-way down into Italy for 15 minutes starting on the hour. (On the half hour coming up from Italy.) (See Trip 53.)

Sweep down off the mountain. In about 23 kilometers, cross the main valley east-west road by jogging a few hundred meters west and then turning down through the village, **Olang** (Valdora, in Italian). Then you're climbing the one-lane **Furkel Sattel,** which after field and forest and a ski tow, comes down to **St. Vigil.** Turn downstream northwest (upstream dead-ends) to **Zwischenwasser** (Longega in Italian) where in a tight little valley our road meets the main north-south road. Turn south, upstream, toward Corvara for only one kilometer, then take the little bridge that crosses the adjacent stream, west, signed "Welschellen." After about ten kilometers of one-lane, the road meets the one-lane "main" **Wurz Joch** road (Trip 42) coming up from St. Martin. Climb the sweepers and hairpins of the Wurz Joch, past the attractive rifugio at the top.

About eight kilometers west of the rifugio, the one-lane forks. The north tine goes down to Brixen. Take the south, the left tine, down to **St. Peter.**

At St. Peter is a Tiroler hotel restaurant with a plaza terrace just as the road hairpins around a building. **Hotel Kabis;** I-39040; Vilnoss; phone: 047 284-0126; fax: 047 284-0395. (The area is called Vilnoss, Funes in Italian.) Here, as all across the Sud Tirol, the hotel and plaza will be full of locals in special Tirolian costume on Sunday morning.

From St. Peter it's but nine kilometers down west to the main valley canyon. Cross under the Brennero Autostrada, over the river, and go south, toward Bozen for a whole eight kilometers of two-lane road. (Coming eastbound from the autostrada, be sure to turn north at St. Peter. The turn is signed "Wurz Joch." Straight ahead dead-ends.)

At **Ponte Gardena,** after eight kilometers of two lane, take the one lane west to and through **Barbian.** From Barbian, it's one lane southerly (two-way) traversing the edge of the mountain to Lengmoos. Along the way are some strange formations below the road: pointed peaks with rock caps.

Lengmoos has a popular restaurant terrace, the Sporthotel Spogler. From Lengmoos it's two lanes to Klobenstein where there's a good hotel, the **Dolomitenblick;** I-39054 Klobenstein; phone: 047 135-6367; fax: 047 135-6503. As its name suggests ("blick" is German for view), the hotel has views of the Dolomites, across the great canyon that contains the Brennero Autostrada way down below.

From Klobenstein, there's a two-laner down to Bozen in the valley. Don't take it. Take the one lane across the mountain to Wangen, a high point in the area with more views of field and forests and Dolomites. A hotel at **Ritten** is the **Berg Gasthof Plorr;** I-39050 Oberrin 45; phone: 047 160-2118.

Twist down to Saren Tal—the Penser Joch road (Trip 33). Turn south downstream to Bozen. (Coming the other way, from Bozen, the turn up the mountain is marked "Ritten".)

In just about eight kilometers, after some tunnels, there's a castle on a pinnacle called Runkelstein. Just past Runkelstein, before Bozen, there's a turn up and west marked "Jenesian" (Genesio in Italian). Take it up the mountain, past **Jenesian** to Molten (Moltina in Italian). Stay up on the mountain heading north to Hafling (Avelengo in Italian). Then it's two lanes down to Meran. There's no way but to wend through Meran to the Passer Tal, the road to St. Leonhard, and the Timmels Joch (Trip 31).

St. Leonhard is a Tiroler style village lined with several hotels and restaurants and it's where the Timmels Joch road and the Jaufen Pass roads meet.

At the fork in the road, the easterly fork is the Jaufen. Take the westerly one, which seems to go down along the rushing river. It's the Timmels Joch road. Once down along the river, there's a bridge across it. Take it. This is the beginning of a remarkable one lane steep climb through forests to a community called Moos. From Moos, it's possible to cross the raging stream and continue the one lane climb up the Timmels Joch to Austria and the Tirol.

Trip 35   Adamello Brenta National Park

Distance	*135 kilometers, with an additional 40 into Lago di Tovel*
Highlights	*Rural Italy with orchards and forests and views of the national park. Passo di Palade (Gampen Joch in German) 1518 meters; Lago di Tovel (1177 meters), a mountain gem with red water, peaks of the national park, Adamello Brenta*
Terrain	*Comfortable two lane road, moderate curves*

The valley roads and autostrada connect Merano with Riva, to its south. This way is more fun.

Leave Merano through the town just southwest of it, Lana, and the Gampen Joch (Trip 29). Across the Joch, there's no more Sud Tiroler culture. It's pure Italian. From Fondo, head on south to Sanzeno where there's a pleasant Italian style hotel-restaurant, the **Albergo la Mela d'Oro** (the golden apple); I-38010 Sanzeno; phone: 04 633-4384.

Next to the hotel is a rural church and beside it, a small war memorial monument in a contemporary style. Most every village in Europe has a war memorial honoring the local dead. This one recalls "the martyrs of the whole world." Nice thought. Southwest of Sanzeno, deep in the mountains of the Adamello Brenta National Park, is a lovely secluded Alpine lake with unique red water reflecting the surrounding peaks.

To find it, go south of Senzano about four kilometers, then westerly about six kilometers to Tuenno where the road into the park and lake is marked. The road ends at the lake, about twelve kilometers upstream from Tuenno. There is a visitor's center, but no services. The park is reported to have bears.

Back at Tuenno, head south for Molveno. Since the main roads tend toward the Brennero Autostrada, it's necessary to avoid it by making several turns in a westerly direction back into the mountains toward Molveno. Molveno is a nicely sited Italian mountain-lake resort with hotels and restaurants well off the foreign visitor routes. There's the **Hotel Belvedere;** I-38018 Molveno; phone: 04 6158-6933; fax: 04 6158-6044. The road around the west side of Molveno's lake is not paved.

South from Molveno the main road hangs high on a cliff edge and then descends into Ponte Arche where there are signs for Riva.

To come the other direction, north from Riva, follow signs for Ponte Arche, the high road, and then on to Molveno.

Riva and Lago di Garda

The south end of long Lake Garda, **Lago di Garda** (Italians are very casual about whether it's *del* or *di* Garda), is down in the flats of the Po Valley of Italy, near historic cities like Verona and Mantova. But the north end is up in the Alps, surrounded by giant vertical cliffs and snowy mountains. At the north point of the lake, surrounded by the cliffs of the Alps, is **Riva,** a small town and a beautiful destination.

Riva is a small lakeside resort, popular with Germans, and with all the amenities needed to serve the traveler—lots of shops, hotels, and restaurants stuffed inside some small fortifications of the Middle Ages. It is only 20 kilometers west of the Brennero-Modena Autostrada, and about 80 kilometers south of Bolzano, but a world away in spirit. It is signed from the autostrada at Rovereto, but it's a lot more fun to come down from the northwest, through Tione and over **Passo Durone.**

Coming from the Dolomites, follow the route that goes down and around **Trento** from **Passo Manghen.** On the loop

Riva sits at the north end of Lago di Garda, surrounded by high Alps and twisting roads. The road hugging the west shore of the lake is often in a tunnel chiseled through high cliffs that rise straight from the lake.

around Trento there are signs for Riva. Riva has a couple of motorcycle shops.

From Riva, there's a shoreline road around the lake that winds for miles through tunnels in the cliffs that rise a thousand feet or so out of the water. The road is in tunnels more than in daylight. Every driveway and intersecting road must be chiseled from the granite. Every spot where a wheel can fit has a restaurant or a hotel. One town, Campione, has a complete interchange tunneled into the adjoining mountain.

A road climbing west right out of Riva at the town's hydroelectric plant is literally a groove cut in the cliffs. Its function as a through road has been recently replaced by a long tunnel, but it provides great views of Riva—the "wind-surfing capital of the world"—and the strange tilt-up strata beside the town that looks like a giant had played with it.

Lake steamers and hydrofoils come into Riva at a pedestrian square with lots of gelaterias. This is where elaborate concoctions are to be consumed leisurely, taking time to indulge in that great European sport, people watching. The sport is European, but Italians are the champions.

Traffic doesn't loop in Riva. It sort of gets shoved away from the lakefront on roads that don't seem to be going in the right direction. Keep an eye on those round, blue signs with white arrows showing which way it's legal to go.

Right on the pedestrian square is Hotel Sole, completely modernized on the inside, some rooms facing the lake; **Hotel**

The main road climbing the cliffs from Lago di Garda to Pieve is either hanging on a ledge or tunneling through a mountain. Honking is okay on blind, narrow corners.

Sole; Piazza 3 Novembre 35; I-38066 Riva del Garda; phone: 046 455-2686; fax: 046 455-2811. The piazza is not always open to vehicle traffic. Some fast talking and Italian arm waving might be called for to reach the hotel. Just don't hit a pedestrian. Next door on the lake is **Hotel Bellavista;** Piazza C. Battisti 4; I-38066 Riva del Garda; phone: 046 455-4271. Approach it by vehicle from the other side.

More modest, facing the same plaza as the Sole is **Hotel Centrale;** I-38066 Riva del Garda; phone: 046 455-2344; fax: 046 455-2138.

A well-known motorcycle journalist and connoisseur rates highly the cuisine at the hotel atop Passo San Giovanni (287 meters!) a couple of kilometers east of Riva on the main road connecting to the Brennero autostrada at Rovereto. And the hotel has rooms and a pool. **Hotel San Giovanni;** phone and fax: 046 454-0101.

It's possible to stay way up atop **Monte Bondone,** northeast of Riva. The roads up are worth the trip. From Riva it's a sweeping dream. Down the far side to Trento it's too many hairpins to count. At almost 1500 meters is **Hotel Montana;** I-38040 Monte Bondone; phone: 046 194-8200; fax: 046 194-8177.

Or try the exotically sited Hotel Paradiso high atop the cliffs on the west side of Lago di Garda (Trip 36).

The balcony of the Hotel Paradiso hangs way out a thousand feet or so over Lago di Garda. It's worth a visit.

Trip 36   Pieve and Passo di Tremalzo

Distance   *About 85 kilometers*

Terrain   *Gentle lakeshore with tunnels, steep, very narrow gorge, and dark tunnels; steep, rocky, unpaved section between Vesio and pass, smooth sweeping asphalt around Lago di Ledro*

Highlights   *Scenic lakeshore, exotic gorge and views from heights, rugged unpaved mountain climb, pass-top rifugio,* ★ ★ *Pieve and Passo di Tremalzo (1894 meters) and Lago di Ledro*

Sited on the tip top of the 1,000-foot cliff, straight up over the lake with a balcony cantilevered into space, is Hotel Paradiso at **Pieve.** And the road to it is an absolute must. Follow the west shore road south about five kilometers past Limone, where the road suddenly opens up with no houses or businesses in sight. Take the 90-degree turn into a tunnel. The road climbs out of the tunnel, makes several hairpins, and goes in another long tunnel—parts of it in full width, parts in tight, narrow curves—to reach a narrow gorge with overhanging cliffs, dripping water, a grotto to the Madonna, and a little monument to Winston Churchill, who must have painted there. Honk the horn on one-lane blind corners. Traffic is two-way, but there's space for only one lane.

The road circles around at a little opening in the cliffs and crosses over itself. At that spot is a good restaurant specializing in trout—pick yours out of the tank.

In another couple of kilometers, at the top of the cliffs, is the village of Pieve. The uphill road from the traffic circle at the gas station climbs past the town piazza, church, and school, and there's the Hotel Paradiso, down a long drive to the cliff's edge. Swimming pool, tennis, and food.

Once, a group of Americans at the Hotel Paradiso was supplied a menu in English. "What's this item, creamy noodle?" they asked. The hostess got out her Italian-English dictionary, which clearly translated "lasagna" into English as "creamy noodle." If you're lucky, they'll have "creamy noodle" as the first course.

If you stop just to look—and you should not miss it—buy something to eat or drink. **Hotel Paradiso;** I-25010 Pieve di Tremosine; Lago di Garda; phone: 036 595-3012; fax: 036 591-8090.

Passo di Tremalzo from Pieve has become a dual-purpose legend since it was featured in *Motorrad,* the German motorcycle magazine. BMW has been seen testing new GS models in the area. The road up the pass is narrow, rocky, and unpaved, with hairpins hanging in space. A riding miscalculation could have very unsatisfactory results. It's not for uncertain riders, but all sorts of persistent street bikes have conquered it. Some may be happier going up it than down.

To find the pass from Pieve (not every intersection is marked), follow the signs from the gas station toward Vesio. The first several kilometers into a narrowing valley from Vesio are paved.

About halfway up, in a grove of trees, the pass road makes a hairpin into a fork going straight ahead, with some signs reading *vietato,* "forbidden." Whether or not it's forbidden, the straight-ahead fork isn't the right road.

At the top of the Tremalzo there's a good rifugio, and the other side, the north side, is all smooth, sweeping asphalt.

The asphalt descent from the rifugio ends on the **Lago di Ledro** road. It swoops around the lake of that name, and starts to descend the cliffs into Riva. That's where the old road's been replaced with a 90-degree sharp turn into the mountain and a tunnel several kilometers long into the back side of Riva.

Public pressure is being exerted to close the unpaved portion of Tremalzo to motorcycles.

Trip 37 The High Road West

· ·

Distance	*About 230 kilometers to Morbegno*
Terrain	*Three narrow, steep, paved, high passes; and three less high*
Highlights	*Rushing streams and high meadows with no traffic, rustic rifugios, ★ ★ Passo di Croce Domini (1943 meters), ★ Passo di Vivione (1828 meters), Passo di Presolana (1294 meters), Col di Zambla (1257 meters), ★ Passo di San Marco (1992 meters)*

A high route west from Riva uses remote passes known and used mostly by locals. Even those persistent explorers, German motorcyclists, seldom venture this way. This route crosses three high ridges between several roughly parallel valleys running south out of the Alps.

Cross the first ridge via the Lago di Ledro road out of Riva, going through the long tunnel, past the Passo di Tremalzo turnoff, and across to **Storo** in the next valley.

Storo appears a drab country village, but it has a first class coffee house that would do any city proud. It has marble and stained glass and comfortable booths and tables. It's at the main village intersection where a small road heads south.

From Storo, eight kilometers south on the valley road alongside a small lake, Lago d'Idro, the **Passo di Croce Domini** road intersects in a 170-degree right turn. After some heavy-duty climbing, you'll reach the mountain village of

Bagolino, hung on steep slopes. It has a nice little piazza with a bakery/coffee shop. The outdoor tables have a view of the gorge and mountains, and the handsome colonnaded village church and campanile above.

From Bagolino, the Croce Domini road becomes one lane of dancing and climbing asphalt that runs beside torrents of water and rises out of the forests to cross the top above the tree line. The rifugio at the top serves refreshments in front of, or practically inside, a giant fireplace.

A short distance from Riva is the tiny mountain village of Bagolino, with a tasty bakery and bar. It's a good stop before tackling the narrow, twisting heights of Passo di Croce Domini.

Passo Vivione is so devoid of traffic that it's easy to conclude there's nobody else on the road.

The dirt road south from the Croce Domini rifugio is not recommended. The road down west from the rifugio has had problems with avalanches and slides, but has always been open to motorcycles. If the rifugio's family is absent, there are a couple of satisfactory mountain albergos just a couple of kilometers down the road.

Breno is a pretty big town at the western base of the Croce Domini. The valley north from Breno is surprisingly industrial (for a narrow Alpine valley), but it's only 20 kilometers to the **Passo di Vivione,** one of the most ignored delights of the Alps. Passo di Vivione starts westerly at **Forno d'Allione.** The pass road turns down across the valley stream, past a smelter furnace. Since *forno* means "kiln" and "furnace" as well as "oven," the turn is well named. In fact, the pass road is inconspicuous around and beyond the parking lot of the smelter. The pass is one-lane, paved, and devoid of traffic.

The little ristorante just across from the smelter is delightful. At this ristorante, the cook is also a wood carver, delighted to show off both his skills. Take note that in all of Italy, the large noon meal, usually more than a lunch, is over by 2:00 p.m. and the kitchen is closed. Because the pass has so little traffic, it's easy to assume you can play on all of its one lane. But there can be other vehicles.

There's a rifugio at the top of the pass, usually run by a little old man. From it are views of empty valleys and jagged mountain peaks.

The pass comes down on the southwest to **Schilpario,** a ski resort. Below Schilpario, resist the temptation to turn down into the deep valley. Rather, stay on the higher road which leads right up **Passo di Presolana,** in the direction of **Bergamo.** The road passes through a resort area popular with Italians, but unknown to most foreigners. There are several good hotels and ristorantes in towns like Rovetta and Clusone, but no English is spoken.

Five kilometers below Clusone, just below the village of **Ponte Nossa,** the **Col di Zambla** road climbs west, while the valley road continues to the large city of **Bergamo.** (Bergamo was home to Montessori and is home to Acerbis.) The Col di Zambla road comes down in the next valley by **Terme San Pellegrino.** Terme means spa or "bad." This is the San Pellegrino of bottled water, often rated the best of bottled waters (better than Perrier?). The bottles and their plastic carriers and the trucks hauling it all will be in evidence. The spa itself looks well past its prime. The International Six-Day Trials were once held in the area.

Passo di San Marco is a rarity: no other bikes. It's not marked. Follow the valley north from San Pellegrino, taking the forks toward the town of **Mezzoldo** (some maps erroneously show the pass from the area of a town called Cusio, but that's the wrong valley). The high road from Mezzoldo is the pass. It crosses over and comes down into the town of **Morbegno** in the Adda Valley (the valley that could be seen from Passo dell'Aprica, upstream from Lago di Como). From Morbegno, there are good connections into Switzerland via the Splugen Pass and the Bernina Pass. (See Trip 27, Maloja Pass, Splugen Pass, etc., and Trip 29, Italian Connections.)

Trip 38   The Low Road West

• •

Distance   *About 210 kilometers to Morbegno*

Terrain   *Three modest passes; occasional hairpins and grades, mostly main roads*

Highlights   *Faster route west than Trip 31, more interesting than autostrada in Po Valley; Passo Durone (940 meters), Passo Campo Carlo Magno (Madonna di Campiglio) (1682 meters), Passo del Tonale (1883 meters), Passo dell'Aprica (1176 meters)*

Taking the higher road north from Riva to Ponte Arche and over Passo Durone to Tione leads to the north-south **Passo Campo Carlo Magno** (that's Italian for Charlemagne) and the ski area Madonna di Campiglio, both in the woods, under the tree line.

At Dimaro, the pass road intersects with the westbound road over **Passo del Tonale,** a barren pass with a World War I *sacrario* (cemetery). The Tonale road comes down to **Ponte di Legno** (the base of Passo di Gavia in Trip 30), and from there to Edolo and over Passo dell'Aprica toward Switzerland at the Bernina. (See Trip 29.)

The Dolomites

· ·

The Italians call them Dolomiti, and the Germans, Dolomiten. Whatever they're called, the first view of the **Dolomites** will take your breath away. No matter how many mountains you've seen, no matter how many times you may have seen the Dolomites, that first glimpse—maybe as you emerge from a tunnel, or maybe as you accelerate out of a hairpin—will be an almost religious experience. The vertical massifs set in feathery green forests are duplicated nowhere. And there are more good roads than a good rider can cover in a week of hard riding.

Draw a straight line on the map between Venezia (Venice) and Munchen (Munich). There in Italy, just below the middle of that line, are the Dolomites. They're east of that giant canyon known as the **Brenner Pass,** the great divide made by the **Adige River** which is used as the major and lowest north-south route across the Alps.

There are good low-level routes around the Dolomites, so no one has to go through them to get anywhere. The only people there are there because of them. The Dolomites are a skier's and motorcyclist's dream.

The Dolomites are in Italy, with Italian laws, stamps, and money, but it was not always thus. Until World War I, they were in Austria, part of the Tirol. The Austrians were on the Germans' side in World War I, and the Italians were on the Allied side. The Austrian and Italian generals ordered up battles much like the horrible ones in France, only these were in the mountains. Little known in our history books are the costly battles fought between Austria and Italy in the Dolomites. Once one side or the other had charged up or down a mountain at great loss of life, they had to build a road to supply the dearly bought area. They built roads and tunnels that didn't seem to go anywhere except to serve some strategic need of the moment.

Now those roads make up a fantastic network for motor-cycle exploring. Besides the roads, the war left only *sacrarios* (cemeteries) and some huge stone forts.

History doesn't indicate that the costly battles in the Dolomites decided anything, but at Versailles the victorious allies awarded the Sud Tirol (South Tyrol) to Italy. In the 1920s, some of the Tirol voted to return to Austria. The rest, including the great Dolomite range, is now known in Italy as the Alto Adige. Some of the World War I monuments and cemeteries (sacrarios) are mentioned on the trips here.

Vast areas of the region still remain Germanic. Many towns have Austrian-style buildings and food and are known by their German names. Typically, one side of a pass, usually the south and east side, will be completely Italian, while the next village, just a pass away, will be Austrian-Germanic. A quick clue: besides the pictures painted on the sides of the buildings, Austrian villages will have a church with a steeple, while an Italian town will have a church with a campanile.

Whether the village is Italian or Austrian, it'll have fresh pasta and great cappuccino. The Austrian ones will have Wienerschnitzel as well. A hotel or restaurant in either will have a dining room set with fresh linen and glasses, and another with bare tables. A meal may be available only in the room with the tablecloths, but there will always be a cover charge for sitting there. Noon time is siesta time and full meal time in Italy, and pasta is just the first or second course. (If pasta and salad is enough for lunch, make that clear, or the courses will keep coming.)

Cortina d'Ampezzo, usually known simply as "Cortina," is the most famous village in the Dolomites. It's spectacularly set on the eastern edge of the Dolomites and has been the site of winter Olympics. Regularly reviewed in travel magazines, it's the summer resort of choice for the wealthy of Milano. (It's a lot cooler than Milano.) Cortina's central pedestrian zone has pricey shops, and a department store with everything, called the Cooperativa. *The New York Times* once said something to the effect that the place to be seen is the bar of Hotel della Post in Cortina. Motorcyclists have been seen there, and also watching the scene from the narrow terrace in front of the hotel. It's a treat to have a drink, especially if the owner, S. Manijgo, is around to talk about the history of the valley. His family has owned the hotel for more than a century, and he has the photos to prove it. Cortina is nice, but expensive. There's a figure eight loop, lying on its side, in the heart of the Dolomites just west of Cortina. The loop includes six major passes. Just as at Andermatt in Switzerland, it's possible to ride the figure eight and expand into the almost endless variations beyond it without ever coming down into lowlands or big cities.

Each of the villages on the trip has hotels and restaurants, many nicer, and all cheaper, than those in Cortina d'Ampezzo. The middle of the figure eight is Passo di Campolongo, only ten kilometers across. The towns at each end of the pass have good accommodations.

The south anchor of Passo di Campolongo is **Arabba,** a completely Italian town with good food and a variety of comfortable hotels. Tourist Information; I-32020 Arabba; phone: 043 67-9130; fax: 043 67-9130.

Spacious rooms and a parking garage can be found at **Hotel Evaldo,** one of the several hotels in Arabba. It has a sauna and jacuzzi and makes a point of serving motorcyclists. I-32020 Arabba; phone: 043 67-9109; fax: 043 67-9358. Very friendly, but not much English spoken. Demi-pension dinners at the Evaldo include pasta (say tagliatelli or cannel-

This best of all views of Cortina d'Ampezzo, a major resort of the Dolomites, is from the Belvedere at Pocol, a little village on the Passo Falzarego, where it intersects with Passo di Giau. (See Trip 40.)

loni), or aubergine (eggplant), or soup as the first course, then entrecote (steak) or veal, vegetables, salad bar, and dessert.

Above Arabba on the Campolongo road is the **Hotel Olympia;** I-32030 Arabba; phone: 043 67-9135; fax: 043 67-9354. It's a nice place with a pleasant view and it solicits motorcycle business.

Ten kilometers north across Passo di Campolongo, at **Corvara** in Badia (usually called just "Corvara"), things are a bit more Germanic. A variety of hotels includes **Hotel Posta-Zirm,** an old-time place that's been modernized and has grown in all directions to include a lovely dining room, an indoor pool, and a ski lift at the side door. I-39033 Corvara; phone: 047 183-6175; fax: 047 183-6580. Dinners include an elaborate salad bar at the Zirm, a good place to mix the American custom of eating salad before the main course with the European one of having it afterwards. Breakfasts are bountiful by Euro standards.

Very popular with motorcyclists is **Pension La Fontana** in Corvara. The parking lot has metal plates for bike stands. Food in the attractive dining room may be about the best in the Alps. Bountifully and beautifully served. Prices are very reasonable. I-39033 Corvara; phone: 047 183-6000; fax: 047 183-6707. The road up the Passo di Campolongo goes right by it.

An option in Corvara would be a handsome new *albergo* overlooking the village and surrounding massifs: **The Gasthof Alisander;** phone: 047 183-6055; fax: 047 183-6686. (*Gasthof* is usually translated into Italian as *albergo*.)

Right in the center of Corvara is the **Hotel Col Alto,** popular with some motorcycle travel groups. I-39033 Corvara; phone: 047 183-6009; fax: 047 183-6066.

In the fall you may see some *cacciatores* . . . hunters.

No matter how many mountains you've seen, the first glimpse of the Dolomites takes your breath away. It's almost a religious experience. This first view is from Wurz Joch, a pass that climbs out of the great canyon of the Adige river.

The west side of the Passo di Falzarego, part of the "Figure Eight" loop in the Dolomites. These mountains are shaped like no others.

One of the 27 hairpins on the west side of Passo Pordoi, part of the Great Dolomite Road.

Trip 39   Dolomite Figure 8

Distance	*About 90 kilometers*
Terrain	*Climbs and descends with lots of hairpins and switchbacks; some cobblestones*
Highlights	*Six major passes encircle fantastic vertical massifs; many cafes and hotels. Includes: ★Passo di Valparola (2192 meters), ★Passo di Falzarego (2105 meters), Passo di Campolongo (1875 meters), ★Passo di Gardena (Grodner Joch) (2121 meters), ★Passo di Sella (2244 meters), ★Passo Pordoi (2239 meters)*

Passo di Valparola starts just downstream (north) of Corvara about five kilometers, at a village called **La Villa** in Italian and Stern in German. The handy signs for the passes are in distinctive brown color. Towns are in blue. The road goes southeasterly across a stream and climbs though several ski resorts. Near the top is the ruin of a massive World War I fort, set amidst a moonscape of Dolomite rocks and crags. A few kilometers south of the summit, the south end of the pass stops at the summit of **Passo di Falzarego,** with a couple of restaurants, a cable car to a neighboring peak, and a statue of an Italian World War I hero.

To the east, the Falzarego descends in hairpins past magnificent vertical formations toward Cortina. The figure eight goes the other way, westerly, in a series of hairpins and tunnels. But not too far down. It hangs high on the edge of the mountain back toward Arabba, villages and fields a thousand meters below on one side, snow capped massifs on the other, a thousand meters up.

The area is known as the Col de Lana, a World War I battleground. Look way down in the valley below at a sacrario, cemetery, in the shape of a cross.

Along the edge of a tight hairpin is a World War I stone fort. It would seem to command the entire valley. Now it's a restaurant.

The southern legs of the figure eight, the Passo di Falzarego and the **Passo Pordoi,** make up part of the **Great Dolomite Road** which goes east from the Brenner road to Cortina. This is the most touristy part of the Dolomites and the oldest pavement. Still, it's so exciting as to be a must. An occasional tour bus may require every inch of the road to get around a hairpin. Remember, when tempted to duck past a bus, that the rear wheels will track inside of the front. In the Alps when the going gets tight, the descending vehicle is supposed to back up. Tourists are early risers, and are usually off the roads by 4 p.m. The roads and colors are good through the long summer evenings.

Each of the passes on the figure eight has tourist facilities. There are several cable cars to the peaks.

At Arabba, the Falzarego joins the Passo di Campolongo heading north, and the Passo Pordoi, still the Great Dolomite Road, climbing west. Passo Pordoi has 33 numbered hairpins on the east side out of Arabba, and 27 down the west side to **Canazei.**

Before the west base of the Passo Pordoi at Canazei, the **Passo di Sella** starts heading north on the figure eight. All of the massifs are famous for mountain climbing, but the Sella is probably the best known. Usually there will be climbers hundreds of meters overhead and hikers with binoculars watching them from below.

The Sella comes down a bit on the north, only to intersect the **Passo di Gardena** heading east on the figure eight. The passes intersect at a road heading west to the Brenner through the **Val Gardena,** a valley very popular with German tourists, who call it Grodner Tal. The valley is loaded with Germanic hotels, and shops selling copper and leather goods.

About halfway up the west side of the Passo di Gardena is a restaurant with a view terrace. It also rents rooms. It's much nicer than the tourist traps atop the pass. **Restaurant Gerard;** phone: 047 179-5274; fax: 047 179-4508.

The Passo di Gardena's east end is downtown Corvara, where one fork in the Y intersection is the Passo di Campolongo climbing south to Arabba, ten kilometers away.

On the east side of Passo Fedaia, motorcyclists want to take the old road through the Sottoguda gorge, not the new road that only gets a brief view of the gorge from the bridge above. The rest of the new road is in tunnels.

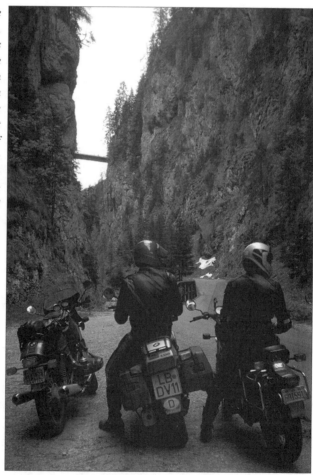

Trip 40 Dolomites: Marmolada

Distance   *About 50 kilometers from Canazei to Pocol*

Terrain   *Steep mountain roads with hairpins*

Highlights   *Almost as fantastic as Trip 39, plus a narrow gorge, all with a lot less traffic. Includes: The Marmolada (Passo di Fedaia) (2057 meters), and ★Passo di Giau (say JOW, rhymes with "how") (2233 meters)*

These passes are east-west connections south of the Great Dolomite Road. They're all Italian, from Canazei at the bottom of the Pordoi on the west, to **Pocol** on the east, just above Cortina on the Falzarego.

Starting east from Canazei, the **Passo di Fedaia** is off the normal tourist route. It climbs the flank of the Marmolada, the largest massif of the Dolomites and the site of some of the bloodiest fighting of World War I. There's a lake at the top of the Fedaia and a ristorante across the dam on the south side of the lake, with views of the massif.

At the tree line on the east side of the Fedaia, the old road descends through a narrow spectacular gorge, only one lane and one vehicle wide. Overhanging rocks obscure the sky. A new highway, built around the gorge, tunnels through the mountain and daylights onto a bridge that crosses the gorge at right angles, only to disappear back into a tunnel on the other side. The view from the bridge is good. The view in the tunnels isn't.

The gorge road is one way, from the bottom up. To get on it from the top, go through the tunnel, across the bridge (stopping to look over the edge) and down into the village, **Sottoguda.** It's a left turn, upstream on cobblestones back into the gorge. Coming up the pass to Sottoguda, go straight through town where the main road goes left. There are picnic tables along the road in the gorge and a small chapel from World War I. A very nice spot.

The area is noted for hand wrought iron work. Some interesting, some weird creations are displayed on buildings in the valley.

Down east below the Sottoguda gorge is the village **Caprile.** There are two twisty roads from Caprile, back north to the figure eight loop. But go past them and through Caprile, and start climbing the wonders of **Passo di Giau,** following signs to Selva di Cadore. First comes a spectacular view area known as Colle Santa Lucia looking to Dolomite peaks and down over feathery forests and a blue lake. Just before Selva, the Passo di Giau road turns up. It's a motorcyclists dream: continuous curves on an alignment laid out in the 1980s. There are a couple of rifugios on Giau, including a handsome new one at the top, the **Cima Passo Giau;** phone: 043 672-0130.

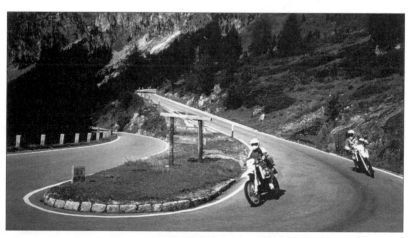

Traffic is permitted only one way at a time on the west side of Staller Sattel, so these bikers can safely plot the line of their choice, using the whole road.

Going into Selva instead of turning up the Giau leads you to **Passo Forcella Staulanza** (1773 meters) and either **Passo Duran** (1601 meters) or **Passo di Cibiana** (1530 meters). From either, main valley roads lead back to the figure eight. The east side of the Giau has some delightful picnic spots.

The Giau comes out on the Falzarego pass road just above Cortina at a small village called Pocol. Here is one of the most impressive World War I monuments and mausoleums in the Alps, and the best view of Cortina. Neither the monument nor the view are visible from the road, and they are not well-marked. To find them, turn up a little driveway just below a big old hotel, usually closed. There's a little sign, *Sacrario.* It's just a hundred meters up the drive to the monument entry gates. They may have an international "do not enter" sign, but the keepers have usually let motorcyclists with respectful attitudes ride in. The monument itself is a church, with the stations of the cross set on each side of a stair cut through the mountain leading to it. The cut frames the monument against the Cortina valley.

The best view of Cortina is from a *Belvedere* (a terrace with a view) just a few meters past the gate to the monument.

The top of Passo di Giau in the Dolomites has a new rifugio and gorgeous views.

Trip 41 Southern Dolomites

Distance	*About 130 kilometers from Arabba (add another 100 to San Baldo)*
Terrain	*Paved mountain roads, some steep tight turns*
Highlights	*Feathery forests, dramatic vertical mountains, little traffic, several rifugios. Includes: Passo Forcella Staulanza (1773 meters), ★Passo Duran (1601 meters), Passo Cibiana (1530 meters), Passo di Valles (2033 meters), Passo di San Pellegrino (1918 meters), Passo di San Baldo (703 meters), Passo di Rolle (1955 meters), Passo di Cereda (1378 meters), Passo di Brocon (1616 meters)*

A 15-kilometer jaunt south, down the valley south from **Caprile,** away from the figure eight, leads to **Cencenighe,** the gateway to **Passo di Valles** and Passo di San Pellegrino. Both go west.

Passo di Valles has a comfortable rifugio at the top with good lasagna. The western slope of Passo di Valles is velvety green. It looks like a park, and it is. Both passes descend deep into the Valle di Fassa, the west extension of the Great Dolomite Road.

The westerly end of the Passo di Valles road is at a T intersection with the **Passo di Rolle** road. Head north at the T to go back to the Great Dolomite Road. Or head south, up and over Passo di Rolle to Fiera, where a northeast turn leads over **Passo di Cereda.** Passo di Cereda has two humps, the lower of which is called **Forcella Aurine.** From the north end of the Cereda, it's possible to head back to the figure eight through Agordo or to continue on over more passes. Passo Duran climbs up to 1601 meters. From the north end of Duran, it's possible to head back toward the figure eight via the Passo Forcella Staulanza, or continue on in the direction of Cortina via the Passo di Cibiana. These passes offer Dolomite type views and usually have little traffic.

To explore farther or to head toward Trento, go south five kilometers from Fiera on the Passo di Rolle road to **Imer.** At Imer, take a road up and west to **Passo di Brocon,** where a rifugio awaits you at the top.

These passes mark the southern edge of the Dolomites. There are some good twisties farther south, and one more pass worth a detour because of the audacity of its construction. Called **Passo di San Baldo,** it crosses a ridge at only 706 meters, not high enough to note otherwise. It's about 15 kilometers southwest of Belluno, one of the major cities south of Cortina, and was the high water mark of the Austrian advance during World War I. The Austrians got down over the ridge in one place, but there was no supply road. So they had to build one. This road is carved out of the cliff face back

Way down south is a pass of amazing audacity: Passo di San Baldo. Each end of each traverse is a hairpin in a tunnel! The tunnels are stacked five or six deep.

and forth. But there was no room for a hairpin at the end of each traverse. So the road goes into the mountain in a tunnel, makes a hairpin, and comes out going the other direction. Then it does the same thing in reverse. The hairpin tunnels are stacked five or six deep, one on top of the other, at each end. They are not lighted!

Once, pulling into Pocol at the east end of Passo di Giau, a rider at the side of the road was studying a map. He was on a Munch, that massive, in-line, four-cylinder machine made in Germany before the Japanese made such a layout their own. "Hey, wait while I get a picture of you and the bike." "Sure, but if you wait a minute there will be a hundred Munchs." And there were.

There are some lovely picnic spots in the Dolomites, for example, this one on the east side of Passo di Giau. (See Trip 40.)

During World War I, the Austrians defended the top of the Passo di Campolongo from the Italians with a massive stone fort, all in a never never land of jagged peaks and boulders. (See Trip 39.)

Trip 42 Adige Canyon

Distance *From Arabba via Wurz Joch, about 60 kilometers to Brixen; via Passo Nigra, about 60 kilometers to Bozen; via Passo di Lavaze and Passo Manghen, about 140 kilometers to Trento*

Terrain *Often narrow, occasionally challenging pass roads. Wurz Joch and Passo Manghen have practically no traffic*

Highlights *A sense of exploring on traffic-free routes to the Brennero Autostrada; ★ Wurz Joch (2002 meters) and ★Passo Manghen (2047 meters) have attractive rifugios. Includes: the Brenner Pass, the canyon of the Adige River, Passo di Costalunga (Karer Pass) (1745 meters), Passo Nigra (Niger Pass) (1688 meters), Passo di Lavaze (1805 meters), Monte Bondone (1537 meters), Passo di Pinei (Panider Sattel) (1437 meters)*

On the great Dolomite passes, even the bottoms of the passes are high. Cortina at the east end is over 1200 meters, and Canazei at the west end is over 1400, so there's still a lot of mountain riding to get to the bottom of things. The great divide, the canyon of the Adige River, home to the Brennero Autostrada, is close to bottom at about 250 meters.

Much of the west end of the Great Dolomite Road has been realigned using tunnels. After a final descent through orchards and vineyards on a road shared with trucks and buses and bicycles and pedestrians, it finally gets down to the Adige River canyon and the autostrada at Ora.

Many alternate roads go up over mountain passes on the way to the Adige, and all of them finally find a tributary gorge to follow down. Better to take one of the up and over and down routes than the Great Dolomite Road.

The most beautiful and most fun motorcycle road between the Great Dolomites and the Adige Canyon is the Wurz Joch, known in Italian as Passo di Erbe. Find it downstream (north) from Corvara, about 15 kilometers north of La Villa and the figure eight. The sign points west to a village across the valley called St. Martin, but there should be a brown sign for Wurz Joch (Passo di Erbe). Above St. Martin, the pass road goes right around a private little castle. (There's another village called St. Martin down the valley north, near Brunico, Bruneck in German. It also has a castle, but it's the wrong St. Martin.)

The pass reaches the Brennero Autostrada in three humps. Wurz Joch is the highest. The road is good as far as the top of the Wurz Joch, where there's an attractive rifugio called Utia de Borz. The deck is a great place to contemplate a first or last view of the Dolomites. West from there, the road is one lane through woods and meadows. Hardly anybody there. When the road splits, follow signs to **St. Andra,** and then on to Milan. There are several attractive hotels around St. Andra, where the road takes up two lanes again.

The pass road gets to the Brennero Autostrada at **Brixen,** a handsome city with shaded streets, squares, and a famous restaurant called **Elefant.** Seems some eastern potentate of the Middle Ages was shipping a prize elephant to the German emperor across the Brenner Pass. The elephant expired in

Brixen. The restaurant named after the unfortunate beast is attractive and has many dining rooms, all different and interesting, some with balconies. The menu is huge, eating there an adventure. Taking the south fork, back above St. Andra leads to St. Peter and the Brennero Autostrada near Ponte Gardena. Going east toward the Dolomites from Brixen, the Wurz Joch is not marked. Follow signs to Milan, a neighboring village, and then to St. Andra. From St. Andra the one-lane road seemingly going downhill is the Wurz Joch road.

Another major access route into the Dolomites from the Brennero Autostrada is the Val Gardena. Unlike the Wurz Joch, the Val Gardena route is well marked from the autostrada. It leads through a popular resort area known to the Germanics as St. Ulrich, and to the Italians as Ortisei. The area is full of hotels. The Val Gardena road ties into the figure eight trip between the Passo di Sella and the Passo di Gardena. A variation is the **Passo di Pinei** (Panider Sattel) south from Ortisei in the Val Gardena.

About 11 kilometers west of Canazei is the turnoff to the north for the **Passo di Costalunga** road. Then, just past the top of the Costalunga, the **Passo Nigra** goes up again, north and west. Both continue down to the Adige Canyon at **Bozen** (Bolzano) on the Brennero Autostrada. The Costalunga (Karer in German) goes down by a small lake, the Karer See, that's famous for its special colors. It's easy to find the lake because of the tour buses. Bozen has all services expected of a major city, including traffic. It's home to Iveco trucks and buses. (See Trip 34.)

Finding the Costalunga and/or the Passo Nigra from the bottom at Bozen requires careful attention. Both take off just north of the city from the old highway that parallels the Brennero Autostrada. There's no connection or marking from the autostrada. The signs are easy to miss among the traffic and commercial activity of the highway, even though the highway seems to be hugging the edge of high cliffs. It's worth the effort, though, because either of two roads will provide both instant relief from the congestion and some fun riding. The crowds will not be going this way.

Passo di Lavaze is a north-south mountain connection roughly parallel to and east of the Brenner Pass. It starts up and south from the Passo di Costalunga road at a country intersection downstream from the village of Nova Levante (labeled Welschnofen in German). Signs point to Nova Ponente (Deutschnofen). At the top of Passo di Lavaze, an unpaved pass called Passo di Occlini (Grimm Joch) goes westerly. Lavaze is anchored on the south by the town Cavalese on the Great Dolomite Road. Just cross the Great Dolomite Road for a further north-south mountain connection, **Passo Manghen.** Go down into the valley below Cavalese to a village called Molina where the Passo Manghen road heads up a finger canyon. It's about 20 kilometers to the top.

Most experienced Dolomite hands don't know of Passo Manghen, even though it has great riding. It's all one lane wide, but two-way traffic, with tight switchbacks in dark forests. It just makes it out above the tree line. On the south slopes there's a rustic but attractive rifugio called Bar Trattoria Molga-Voltrighetta. The south end of the Manghen is on another main valley road that heads down west to Trento (Trent in German and English), a major city in the Adige Canyon and the Brennero Autostrada.

Maps show Passo Cinque Croci just east of the Manghen. It's not open to the public.

This main valley road to Trento descends and goes around Trento without going into it, crossing the Brennero Autostrada. Then there's signing for Riva del Garda that seems to be going in the wrong direction, but works. The signed route to Riva climbs a new road west out of the Adige valley. The nicest route into Riva is to head west to Ponte Arche and then south.

Or, just a few kilometers up west of Trento, an exciting road into Riva turns sharply uphill, signed Monte Bondone. With too many hairpins to count, it climbs to over 1500 meters, passes Hotel Montana (see hotel listings at the beginning of the chapter on Riva and Lago di Garda), and then swoops and sweeps down to Riva.

Trip 43   Cortina

• •

Distance   *About 40 kilometers to Drei Zinnen; about 120 over Kreuzberg and back*

Terrain   *Irregular sweeping mountain pass roads*

Highlights   *Mind-boggling views from Drei Zinnen (toll); forests, vertical massifs, restaurants and hotels. The trip includes: Passo Tre Croce (1805 meters), ★ Misurina and Drei Zinnen (Tre Cime di Lavaredo) (2320 meters), Passo del Zovo (1476 meters), Passo di Monte Croce (Kreuzberg Pass) (1636 meters), Furkel Sattel (1759 meters)*

Like many European cities, Cortina has a one-way loop street system. Some of the core inside the loop is pedestrian zone. If you miss a stop or turn, the only solution is to go around again. Cortina's loop isn't round—there are some switch-backs and some hairpins—but by the third or fourth circuit, it becomes familiar. In the course of circling Cortina, you'll see brown signs pointing the way to the Passo di Falzarego and to **Passo Tre Croce.** Both start climbing right in the village, the Falzarego westerly, and the Tre Croce easterly.

The Tre Croce is pleasant enough. The prize is Lake Misurina just east of the pass. Its exquisite blue reflects the surrounding Dolomite massifs. There is a bit of en-trepreneurial clutter. On the north side of Lake Misurina, still just minutes out of Cortina, a little road marked *Drei Zin-*

nen and/or *Tre Cime* takes off to the east. It's a dead-end, private toll road that climbs up several hundred meters in a series of hairpins and sweepers that reveal dramatic views of Dolomite crags, the very best view of the Dolomites possible with wheels still on the ground. The cameras will be out.

From **Misurina** north, it's all downhill to **Dobbiaco** (Toblach) and the main roads into Austria.

The roads farther east are not Dolomite dramatic. At **Auronzo** it's possible to go back behind the big domed church and get out of the valley traffic on the **Passo del Zovo.** It heads north and connects with the **Kreuzberg Pass** in the direction of Austria.

The Kreuzberg Pass (Passo di Monte Croce in Italian) has nice hotels and good views of the Dolomites. **Hotel Kreuzberg Pass** has many facilities including an indoor pool. I-39030 Sexten-Hochpuster Tal; phone: 047 47-0328; fax: 047 47-0383. The turn off for the Kreuzberg from Austria is at **Sexten** (Sesto in Italian).

An audacious piece of road that seems without purpose except that it exists can be found east of Auronzo and San Stefano heading south from Campolongo. It's a rough gravel trail up a canyon. Alas, about eight kilometers up, it turns to marvelously engineered asphalt so tightly lapping its hairpins that it looks like a piece of ribbon candy. Turn after tight turn scales the mountain, to end in more rock trail.

North of Corvara, a little-known pass called **Furkel Sattel** cuts across some pleasant mountains. Its chief interest is that it cuts out a bunch of congested valley traffic and makes a direct connection with Staller Sattel, one of the best ways into or out of Austria. From the road north of Corvara, five kilometers downstream from the turnoff to the Wurz Joch at St. Martin, is the village Longega, squeezed in the gorge. That's where the Furkel Sattel road heads up a finger valley. Then at St. Viglio, the pass road goes north. The road straight ahead through St. Viglio dead-ends, but the Furkel Sattel passes some minor ski resorts and some lovely vistas over Tiroler countryside, then comes out on the north at the village Valdaora (Olang in German) on the main road into Austria, and at the south end of the Staller Sattel. (For another way to use the Furkel and Staller Sattels, see Trips 34, 44, and 53.)

Trip 44 Austrian Connections

Distance *About 70 kilometers from Cortina to Austria at Staller Sattel;
about 150 kilometers to Austria at Plocken Pass; about 175 to
Austria at Nassfeld Pass*

Terrain *Exciting climbs by forests and lakes*

Highlights *Green lake, one-lane road on ★ Staller Sattel (2052 meters);
populated valley roads wind to Plocken and Nassfeld Pass (1557
meters). Interesting switchbacks on Plocken Pass (1362 meters),
Sella Ciampigotto (1790 meters), Forcella di Lavardet (1542
meters), Sella di Razza (1760 meters), Passo Zovello (963 meters)*

North of Cortina and about ten kilometers east of Brunico
(Bruneck) at Valdaora (Olang), the Staller Sattel takes off
toward Austria. The intersection is right beside a lumber
yard. The pass road winds through lovely Tiroler fields, past
a glacier blue-green lake, and climbs to the pass in a fun-and-
games, one-way road through the forest. The one-way part is
controlled, so there's 15 minutes for up traffic and 15 for
down, with 15 minutes to clear each way. So there's only 15
minutes an hour to start up or down. The border guards are at
the top to make sure there's no cheating.

About 14 kilometers into Austria, just below the village of
St. Jakob (one of those villages where the road jogs around
an old house), there's a beautiful hotel restaurant right beside

the road called **Tandlerstub'n;** A-9963 St. Jakob. A great place to try Schweinshax'n, a Bavarian and Austrian specialty. The best translation is "hog knuckles" and that falls far short of describing the succulent slices of pork here. The "joint" will be dramatically served on a huge platter with all kinds of trimmings including Semmelknodel, a kind of dumpling.

Two other passes farther east in the Dolomites are useful as escapes from valley highway traffic.

About 75 kilometers east of Misurina, through moderately interesting countryside and the town of Sappada, the **Plocken Pass** makes a dramatic climb into Austria. The Plocken Pass (Passo di Monte Croce Carnico) isn't high, but the switchbacks are dramatic. It's a good gateway to the south end of the **Grossglockner** via the **Gailberg Sattel.** (See Trip 53.) Another 30 kilometers farther east, the **Nassfeld Pass** road climbs quickly into Austria from the autostrada at **Pontebba.** (See Trip 60.)

There's an interesting, occasionally rough little road parallel to the east-west road through Sappada, and just south of it, known as **Forcella di Lavardet.** There are two ways to it, starting in the main valley just downstream from **Auronzo.** (Auronzo has to be one of the longest villages in the Alps. It goes on and on.) The main route goes by the village Larenzago, made famous by the visits of Pope John Paul II. The turnoff is marked "Casera Razzo." (Casera is an Italian army installation). The road climbs ruggedly over a pass called **Sella Ciampigotto,** wends past the usually unoccupied military base at Sella Razzo, then goes over the Forcella di Lavardet. (At this point it meets the other connection.) It's good pavement with lots of markers on down east through forests to **Comeglians.** From there, a road east crosses a low pass (Passo Zovello, 963 meters) to Sutrio, where the Plocken Pass road heads north into Austria.

The other connection from the area of Auronzo is through St. Stefano. At Campolongo this connection heads south, up a rocky valley. Parts are not paved. Then, wonder of wonders, it climbs the mountain side in a stacked series of perfectly matched and paved hairpins, looking something like that hard ribbon Christmas candy. Then it joins the Lavardet road.

▲▲ Liechtenstein

● ●

Liechtenstein is that little, rich country where the prince lives in the castle on the hill and every once in a while they have a skier in the Olympics. About 30 kilometers long and 15 wide, it's sort of in the Alps, using Swiss money, German language, but its own stamps. Switzerland is to the south and west; Austria is to the north and east. The Rhein, flowing north now, marks much of the boundary with Switzerland. This is downstream from the Vorderrhein and the Hinterrhein and the Via Mala and Chur. (See Trips 26, 27, 28.) Just across the Rhein is the Swiss Autobahn. You can get anywhere from Liechtenstein.

Vaduz, the capital, and several other villages in Liechtenstein are pleased to accommodate motorcyclists as well as sell stamps.

From the castle-topped village in the south called Balzers, an interesting road runs through the woods, over a little pass, and through a stone military gate into Switzerland and the cute Swiss village called Maienfeld, leading to Landquart and Wolfgang Pass. (See Trip 28.)

In the middle of the country, starting at **Vaduz** or the village of **Triesen,** a Liechtenstein mountain road climbs to the villages of **Triesenberg** and **Malbun.** Triesenberg hangs high on the mountainside and has gorgeous views of the valley of the Rhein and Schwagalp. Malbun, on through a tunnel from Triesenberg, is in a high ski bowl at about 1600 meters.

The secret way up to Triesenberg and Malbun is the narrow, cliff-hanging, one-way (up only) road that starts at the prince's castle.

At Triesenberg a good hotel is the **Martha Buhler** (named after the skier); FL-9497 Triesenberg; Liechtenstein; phone: 075 262-5777; fax: 075 268-1520. Farther up is **Rizlina Berg Gasthaus,** hung on the edge of the mountain. Same address. phone: 075 262-0224.

One of many hotels in Malbun is the **Montana;** FL-9497 Malbun; Liechtenstein; phone: 075 263-7333; fax: 075 264-2272.

Hotel Landgasthof Schatzman is on the main road in Triesen; FL-9495; phone: 075 392-4222; fax: 075 392-4224. Liechtenstein's Tourist Office is FL-9490 Vaduz; phone: 075 232-1443; fax: 075 392-1618.

About that (FL)? Furst is a German word for prince. So the Principality of Liechtenstein becomes Furstentum Liechtenstein.

Across the Rhein, right on the main drag in **Buchs,** Switzerland, is a Honda dealer, Stricker Motos, that has been very helpful to foreign bikers.

Trip 45 Liechtenstein

• •

Distance	*About 60 kilometers explores the whole country*
Terrain	*A few narrow, one-way roads, some sweeping climbs, a slippery tunnel*
Highlights	*Good views of the Rhein Valley, castles, hotels, restaurants*

By the time you've found the places mentioned in the introduction, you will have seen all of Liechtenstein.

Trip 46 Santis and Schwagalp

Distance	*About 100 kilometers round trip from Liechtenstein*
Terrain	*Gently climbing and sweeping mountain roads*
Highlights	*Less-traveled Switzerland, Chrazeren Pass (1278 meters), Wildhaus (1090 meters)*

A loop climbs through the lower Swiss Alps just across the Rhein from Liechtenstein into the remote little canton of Appenzell. Appenzell has been most famous recently for its method of voting in public meetings, from which voting, women have historically been excluded. Still, it's sort of romantically quaint, with buildings and people that look the way Swiss buildings and people should.

Across the Rhein from Liechtenstein, past the sizable Swiss town of Buchs, at the village of **Gams,** a road climbs west across the south side of Santis mountain. This road with little traffic crosses a minor pass of about 1000 meters at **Wildhaus,** and comes in about 25 kilometers to the village Neu St. Johann.

For more fun, go south of Gams to **Grabs** and take the little one lane road to Grabser Berg and on to Wildhaus. Then at Wildhaus, take the little road south to Schwendi, where there's the **Alpenrose Hotel;** CH-9658 Wildhaus; phone:

071 999-2121; fax: 071 999-1052. The road wanders across the mountain, finally rejoining the main road at **Unterwasser,** right at the fine **Hotel Santis;** CH-9657 Unterwasser; phone: 071 999-2811; fax: 071 999-3474.

From **Neu St. Johann,** a mountain road heads east toward Appenzell over **Chrazeren Pass.** This is no Furka nor Susten Pass, but a forest and meadow road, with some imposing granite peaks around. At the top of the pass, a turnoff leads to the base station of a cable car that goes up the mountain, Santis. For some reason, the parking lot and restaurant at the cable car is a *Tofftreffpunkt.* The road goes on down to Urnasch, then to the town of **Appenzell,** where a small road heads back over a mountain toward the Rhein Valley at Oberriet.

Trip 47   Western Austria

· ·

Distance	*About 260 kilometers*
Terrain	*Some sweeping, some twisting climbs and descents; narrow road on Furka Joch*
Highlights	*Lovely farms, forests, glacier views at ★ Silvretta (2036 meters), hotels, restaurants, ski resorts. Includes: Arlberg Pass (1793 meters), Flexen Pass (1773 meters), Hochtannberg Pass (1679 meters), Faschina Joch (1487 meters), Furka Joch (1761 meters) (Vignettes, stickers, are required to drive on Austrian Autobahns. They can be purchased at most gas station and borders)*

Austria knows how to take care of tourists. Practically every corner has an attractive Gasthaus or hotel, with "Zimmer freis" in between. *Zimmer frei* means "room available," and is the Germanic equivalent of "bed and breakfast." Invariably, they're good and reasonably priced.

The most western state of Austria, called Vorarlberg, and its capital, **Feldkirch,** are right at Liechtenstein, but separated by high Alps from the rest of the country. So it takes some pretty good pass roads to tie Austria together. Since most Alpine pass roads run north-south, these Austrian roads going mostly east-west can be entertaining as well as useful. The main one is the **Arlberg Pass,** now with an Autobahn and a tunnel to take the trucks and buses off the good mountain road. It starts at Feldkirch, which is really on the north border of Liechtenstein. Might as well take the Autobahn from Feldkirch as far as **Bludenz-Ost.** (Don't confuse Bludenz on the Arlberg road with Bregenz, north of Feldkirch on the Boden See, site of popular summer music festivals.)

At Bludenz-Ost, one of the best roads in Austria heads south. Called the **Silvretta Strasse,** it roughly parallels the Arlberg, but takes a rollicking time getting there, so it has only enthusiasts on it. And, welcome to Austria, there's a toll. Austria has a lot of toll roads.

After a short run up a valley past sturdy Austrian farm houses and neatly manicured pastures, and 50 kilometer speed limits seriously enforced, the road has an exciting steep climb with switchbacks and hairpins and views of the same, up to a lake. This is a *Stau See,* a good German word meaning a lake created by a dam. Then there's more climb to a higher lake and the pass, **Bieler Hohe,** where there's a delightful restaurant terrace with views over the lake reflecting snowy peaks.

A refreshing non-alcoholic drink available nowhere but Austria and Bayern (Bavaria) is Spezi (spait zee). It's an orange flavored cola. A big one, a *grosse Spezi,* usually comes in a half-liter beer glass.

From the top, the pass road works down eastward through a pleasant valley. About six kilometers down, there's a side road that climbs up north to another Stau See with a restaurant. On down east, the valley road connects again with the Arlberg road. Just before the junction, there's a good view of a castle and an often photographed high bridge called **Trisannabrucke** that carries the railroad up the Arlberg.

Heading west, back up the Arlberg from the junction, the old road is a good climb that also avoids the toll tunnel under the pass. Watch for the beautiful Austrian farm houses showing considerable pride of ownership. With elaborate corner bay windows, deep arched doors, balconies, and wide, over-hanging roofs, they are often decorated with pictures and maybe poems or historical names in Gothic script. Contemporary ones are of block construction with light beige stucco and dark brown trim. The gable end almost always faces the road. On a pole over the front gable end is a lantern-like bell tower. Some of the lanterns are pretty ornate.

The old road up the pass is okay because the traffic is taking the Autobahn tunnel. Along it are a bunch of saintly towns: St. Jakob, St. Anton, St. Christoph, all of them labeled *am Arlberg* to distinguish them from saintly towns of the same name scattered all over Austria.

Just west of its summit, the Arlberg intersects the **Flexen Pass.** The Flexen heads north in a series of fairly tight sweeps covered by wooden snow sheds hung on the mountain. Just over its top are the famous ski resorts of Zurs and **Lech,** in the valley of the Lech river (Lech Tal) and the Austrian state of Tirol. Both towns have noteworthy buildings decorated with pictures of saints and local heroes, or maybe the building's first owner. The Hotel Post in Lech is particularly nice. (Every town in the Alps has a Hotel Post.) Lech has attractive outdoor restaurant facilities. If tablecloths and umbrellas are out, the place is in operation.

Seven kilometers below Lech, at **Warth,** there's an intersection where the **Hochtannberg Pass** heads northwest. East is the Lech Tal and roads described in Trip 49. Just west of the intersection on the Hochtannberg road is **Hotel Warther Hof;** A-6767 Warth; phone: 055 83-3504; fax: 055 83-4200. It's large and handsome and well known to Edelweiss Tour folk. Its brochures show bikes and bikers.

It's about 23 kilometers westerly over the Hochtannberg to the village of **Au,** where the **Furka Joch** road heads back to **Rankweil** and Feldkirch. (This is Furka *Joch.* Furka *Pass* is at Andermatt, Switzerland, and Furkel Sattel is in the Dolomites.) Above Au, at a village called **Damuls,** a new road heads back to Feldkirch over a pass called **Faschina Joch,** 1487 meters. It's completely roofed with grass growing on top. From above, it looks like a long line of windows.

The Furka Joch, a remote, nobody-takes-it-on-purpose road, goes on through Damuls.

Damuls has a couple of nice hotels. One, the Adler, in a crook of the Furka Joch road, has a good baker as well as a cook. **Hotel Adler;** A-6884 Damuls; Bregenzerwald; phone: 055 10-2200; fax: 055 102-2010. The hotel dates from before Columbus, but has every modern convenience.

Above Damuls, the Furka has some one lane parts. Just east of the summit is a restaurant with a sweeping mountain view, Jagerstuble, advertising good "burger" food—not hamburger food, as well as deer specialties; phone: 055 10-373.

Heading the other way, looking for the Furka Joch and Damuls from Fieldkirch, follow signs first to Rankweil. Here's the best, and almost secret way.

In downtown Feldkirch, just east of the tunnel that takes the main road around the old town is a plaza, platz, with motorcycle parking yet. On the edge of the platz, right where the cobblestoned street is marked for pedestrians only, there's a sign for Gofis. It points up a steep cobbled road. Take it. In a minute you're high above Feldkirch, in fields crossing over everything, including the Autobahn, all down in tunnels below. Gofis is a village on the mountain. From it, more signs point to Rankweil, gateway to the Furka Joch.

▲ Austrian Tirol

Innsbruck is the historic capital of the Tirol, site of Olympics, and a good-sized city that's no fun to drive in or through. Strategically located where the Brenner Pass to Italy reaches the Inn Tal (valley), it's hard to miss. The mountains are so close around that there are no immediate alternative roads. The Autobahn in the Inn Tal goes by Innsbruck hung on the edge of the mountains. It's free and it's the recommended route around Innsbruck. Innsbruck looks nice from the Autobahn. The Brenner Autobahn from Italy makes a T with the one in the Inn Tal at Innsbruck, but it's a toll road.

The Inn River comes down from St. Moritz in Switzerland (see Trips 26–30) and heads easterly through Innsbruck, where there is indeed a *brucke,* a bridge, and finally north to Germany where it flows into what we call the Danube (in German, it's Donau). The Autobahn follows the Inn around to Germany, so while Munchen lies straight north of Innsbruck, the Autobahn connection loops around to the east. The Autobahn remains the fastest way to get to Munchen.

To add to the general geographic confusion, the only Autobahn route from the Tirol in Austria to Salzburg and Wien (Vienna), both also in Austria, goes into and through Germany.

For tourist information about Innsbruck and the immediate area, contact the Tourist Office; A-6021 Innsbruck; Austria; phone: 051 259-850; fax: 051 259-8507.

Imst is a town about 70 kilometers west of Innsbruck in the Inn Tal, where several good pass roads come together. The area is packed with elaborate hotels, comfortable in every aspect, including price. A good hotel in Imst is **Hotel Linserhof;** Teilweise 1; A-6460 Imst; phone: 054 12-2416; fax: 054 126-641-5133. It's several kilometers above Imst on the **Hahntenn Joch** road, well signed, but way back from the road. It has lovely views.

In the tiny village of **Berwang** is a large hotel with all kinds of services, the **Kaiserhof;** A-6622 Berwang; phone: 074 8285.

Or check the hotels listed in Trip 47 at Damuls and Warth, or the ones listed on Trip 48 along the Timmels Joch at Vent and Otz.

Trip 48 Innsbruck Passes

• •

Distance *Via Brenner Pass, about 30 kilometers to Italy; via Timmels Joch, about 100 kilometers to Italy; via Reschen Pass, about 100 kilometers to Italy; about 100 kilometers via Piller Hohe up Kauner Tal*

Terrain *Brenner: low pass, major Autobahn; Timmels Joch: long, sweeping valley to high exotic pass; Reschen: long valley run, low pass; Kauner Tal: steep mountain climb*

Highlights *Brenner Pass (1374 meters) quick route to Italy (toll), fantastic bridges; Timmels Joch (2509 meters): nice valley villages, sweeping climb to high mountains (toll); Piller Hohe (1558 meters), Kauner Tal (2750 meters), Reschen Pass (1504 meters) (no toll) leads to Passo dello Stelvio*

It's a short, quick run, less than 50 kilometers, over the Brenner Pass from Innsbruck to the area of the Italian passes around Merano (see Trips 31–35) and the Dolomites (Trips 39–44). That's the Brenner's chief merit. But it's so low and so congested that it hardly deserves other comment.

There is a *Bundesstrasse,* a non-freeway, non-toll, federal road, across the Brenner alongside the Autobahn. It has usually been the choice of motorcyclists. From it, the gigantic structures of the Autobahn, including the famous **Europabrucke bridge,** look awesome. But the road goes through a picturesque town called Matrei am Brenner with one narrow street that has tried to outlaw motorcycles. Various courts are hearing various appeals of the arbitrary decision. The only way around Matrei is the toll Autobahn. So far, motorcycles are legal.

About thirteen kilometers up Stubai Tal, a dead-end finger valley, west off the Autobahn at the famous Europabrucke, is the motorcycle friendly **Hotel Capella;** at Neustift; phone: 052 26-2515; fax: 052 262-5155.

If there's time, it's more fun to take the Timmels Joch rather than the Brenner Pass, or even the Reschen Pass. The Timmels Joch (its other end is described in Trip 31) parallels the Brenner starting about 45 kilometers west of Innsbruck, near **Kuhtai** and **Haiming** (Trip 49). It climbs south up the Otz Tal, through the town, **Otz,** where there's the large comfortable old time **Hotel Post** (of course); A-6433 Otz; phone: 052 52-6303; fax: 052 52-2176. Further up the Otz Tal at Zwieselstein, a finger valley called Vent Tal climbs up west. At the end is another **Hotel Post;** A-6458 Vent; phone: 052 54-8119; fax: 052 548-1194. It's at almost 1900 meters and sports a small indoor pool looking out at glaciers.

The Reschen Pass (see Trip 32) starts up out of the Inn Tal at **Landeck,** about 75 kilometers west of Innsbruck. It's mundane, lower, and a bit more of a detour than the Timmels Joch. A good way to get to the Reschen is to head south, up and out of the Inn Tal from Imst, short of Landeck, over a little-known pass, **Piller Hohe,** and come out on the Reschen Pass at Fliess or **Prutz.** Little Piller Hohe allows the rider to sail along the high mountain, occasionally looking down on the traffic in the Inn Tal. From Prutz a road up the dead end Kauner Tal valley leads to a *Stau See* and one of the highest roads in Austria. The upper part has a toll.

Trip 49 Obscure Tiroler Roads

Distance	*About 250 kilometers*
Terrain	*Some sweeping, some tight, narrow mountain roads*
Highlights	*Famous castles, churches, little-used mountain roads, nice restaurants and hotels. Includes: Ammer Sattel (1118 meters), Berwang (1336 meters), ★Hahntenn Joch (1894 meters), ★Haiming Joch (1685 meters), ★Kuhtai (2017 meters), Seefeld in Tirol; Telfs; Holzleitner Sattel (1126 meters), Fern Pass (1209 meters)*

In Ober Bayern (southern Bavaria), the mountains and roads are exciting when compared to the Great Plains, but the real riding is readily available in the high Alps of the Austrian Tirol just across the border. This trip is easily accessible from Munchen as well as **Oberammergau** and **Garmisch,** and anywhere in the Tirol.

Starting from the town of **Ettal,** just outside Oberammergau and just north of Garmisch, escape the traffic and tourists by turning south over the **Ammer Sattel.** Ettal has a huge domed baroque monastery church right near the intersection. Apparently the monks make good brandy, and the handsome gold and white interior of the church has consumed some of the profits. The interior is spectacular in gilt and white with plenty of baroque cupids hanging around the pillars and over pictures, and with a celestial dome, all in the style of the mid-1700s. Some exterior traces of the original Gothic building (like the front doorway) are still visible. Worth a visit, and it's free. Park close, at the east end of the lot, in front of the shops.

The turn for the Ammer Sattel is marked with signs for the **Konigschloss Linderhof,** one of Mad King Ludwig's castles which is ten kilometers up the road. The German noun *Schloss* is almost always translated to the English word "castle." This can be misleading, because Schloss can also mean "palace." (No walls or battlements on a palace; a castle may have a moat and other fortifications.) This Konigschloss, royal castle, is Ludwig's small baroque jewel of a palace, with a jet fountain and an underground lake for Wagnerian opera, built in the late 19th century. It can't be seen from the road. Tours take a couple of hours.

Ludwig was king of Bayern in the days that Bismarck was uniting Germany under a German, rather than an Austrian Kaiser. Ludwig's sympathies were with the Austrians, which as it turned out, was unfortunate. Meantime, he built two other castles besides Linderhof to play in: **Neuschwanstein** is the turreted wonder on every travel poster, near Fussen and Reutte; and **Herrenchiem See**, on an island in a lake named Chiem See, between Munchen and Salzburg. Of course, he had inherited other castles and palaces. Neuschwanstein was the inspiration for Disney's Magic Kingdom castle. Herrenchiem See on the island is supposed to look like the French Chateau of Versailles. It's necessary to take a ferry to Herrenchiem See.

Past Linderhof, the Ammer Sattel road goes through a forest and climbs to the low Sattel which happens to be the Austrian border. Into Austria a few kilometers, the road winds around an Alpine lake called Plan See, with a nice hotel at the end of the lake closest to the border and several serviceable restaurants. Then it makes a rather windy, steep descent into **Reutte** (say "Roy tuh"), a bustling Tiroler town. Reutte has a two-lane Autobahn around it which can seem confusing. Follow signs south toward **Lermoos** and **Fern Pass,** away from Germany (D), and exit in a couple of kilometers at **Bichlbach** and head for Berwang and **Namlos.** This is delightful rural Tirol. Some of the road is barely one lane, dancing around high Alpine meadows. Berwang has nice-looking hotels. (See the listing at the beginning of the chapter.)

The road comes down in the Lech Tal (the valley mentioned in Trip 47). Five kilometers west up the Lech Tal at **Elmen** is the obscure turnoff for a great, usually ignored pass, the Hahntenn Joch. The narrow road crosses a little field and then starts climbing the rock face in a long steep traverse before turning into a high valley for some more twisting fun. There are no facilities at the top, which has a huge slope of sliding alluvial granite, but short of the top is a cute Gasthaus named **Zur Gemutlichkeit;** A-6644 Bschlabs 31; Lech Tal; Tirol; phone: 056 35-259; fax: 056 35-521. (How many other towns start with five consonants?) It faces an equally cute onion-domed church. Prices at Zur Gemutlichkeit are very reasonable.

The narrow road comes down through the woods, past the **Hotel Linserhof,** into Imst, another prosperous Tiroler town with a typical Austrian church. Bavarian churches typically have onion domes on the tower. Austrian churches, like that at Imst, have a square tower with a clock face on each side, then an open belfry topped with four gables finished off with a tall pointed steeple.

Imst, like Reutte, has a sort of two-lane bypass Autobahn around it, connecting with the major east-west Autobahn in the Inn Tal between the Arlberg and Innsbruck.

Head toward Innsbruck about ten kilometers to a small village named Haiming. Haiming is a marked Autobahn Ausfahrt (exit). Opposite the village, heading south up the mountainside, is the Haiming Joch road. It's hardly more than a driveway. The signing is to **Ochsengarten.** This narrow, one-lane road climbs past steep fields, with little haystacks and occasional Zimmer Frei signs, a Gasthaus and a delightful new hotel with a view of the whole valley: **Hotel Ferien-schlossl;** A-6425 Haimingberg, Tirol; phone: 52 669-7178; fax: 52 669-71787. Past the hotel, the road climbs into a high forest, and then comes down just a bit to the Kuhtai road at the intersection called Ochsengarten.

Kuhtai is a high pass, but for some reason it's never called a pass, just Kuhtai. It goes east-west, roughly parallel to the Arlberg-Innsbruck Autobahn down in the Inn Tal, but higher in the Alps. Even though it's close to such traveled ways and to Innsbruck, it never has traffic. At Ochsengarten, it seems hardly more prominent than the tiny Haiming Joch road.

West from Ochsengarten, the Kuhtai road makes a steep descent to **Otz,** on the Timmels Joch road. Kuhtai, the pass, is the other way, east and up over the tree line past a massive earth dam and its lake. There are a couple of ski hotels at the top. And a "Bike Stop," on the north side of the road. You have to go in. The interior is a delight, and so is the staff. Nothing wrong with the outdoor view terrace, either.

Then a fairly modern road sweeps down east in a long valley called the Sellrain Tal. Some straights end in rather abrupt tight corners through villages, including Gries, with attractive **Hotel Antonie;** A-6182 Gries; phone: 052 362-03271; fax: 052 362-0349. Then the road enters a tight gorge shared with a raging mountain torrent, exiting without further ado in the Inn Tal, at a village named **Kematen,** just a couple of kilometers from downtown Innsbruck.

Here, the secret is to go straight ahead through Kematen and under the Autobahn, and sweep up the mountain on the north side of the Inn Tal. This is the main *Bundesstrasse* (federal road) toward Garmisch in Germany. But up the mountainside a few kilometers, still in Austria, is the exit for Seefeld. Seefeld is famous for cross-country skiing. Guess that means it's flat on top. West of Seefeld, a delightful little road hung on the mountainside heads for the Tiroler town of Telfs. Straight on through Telfs toward **Holzleitner Sattel,** the road passes through **Mieming,** known to many motorcycle tour-takers as the home of Edelweiss Bike Travel.

The west side of the Holzleitner has wonderful, wide sweepers down to the picturesque village of Nassereith. But first, on the way down, pause to view the lush green Tiroler valley below. Often there's a vendor selling *heiss Wurst und Brot,* the Tiroler equivalent of a hot dog, only better. A good munch helps you contemplate the view. (Sometimes "heiss wurstl" gets translated, "hot sausage." In this instance, it's hot, cooked, not HOT HOT.)

North from Nassereith is the **Fern Pass,** a nice road, with too much traffic and too many anxious drivers, that fortunately isn't too long. There's a Gasthaus at each side of the top, both with elaborate painted scenes on the exterior walls. The southern one has historical pictures, including the arrival of American tanks near the end of World War II, with the building in flames.

Even though it's pretty low by Alpine standards, the Fern Pass is the closest mountain pass for many Germans, and always has a lot of tour bus traffic. To accommodate all the traffic, the north side has new tunnel work that leads quickly toward Lermoos and back to Germany at Garmisch, or on to Reutte.

Just across the German border from Reutte is **Fussen,** and Ludwig's castle **Neuschwanstein,** alongside the older castle, **Hohenschwangau.**

If there's time for one Bayrisch baroque church, choose the one at Rottenbuch, just a few kilometers north of Oberammergau. It's just off the main road through a low arch gate. Typically, baroque churches are very plain on the outside with no stained glass. But the inside of Rottenbuch is astonishing. Elaborate carving and plaster detail have run riot. It's delightfully flamboyant. The frescoes cast a rosy glow, much cozier than the famous Wies Kirche only ten kilometers away. Tours never go to Rottenbuch, probably because buses can't get through the village gate.

Deutsche Alpenstrasse

The southern border of Germany, and of Bayern, is where the Alps begin. The big stuff is all south of Germany. In fact, the Zugspitze, the highest point in Germany, is on the Austrian border.

In fits and starts, Germany has been constructing a road along the border, called the Deutsche Alpenstrasse. Little of it bears comparison with the high Alps. But a few parts are interesting and are popular with German motorcyclists. The best part by far is a little loop, the **Rossfeldringstrasse** on the mountain above **Salzburg** and **Berchtesgaden.**

As a well-promoted vacation area, the Bayern region is full of hotels and restaurants. One less-trafficked village is **Lenggries,** northeast of the town of Garmisch-Partenkirchen, and just a few kilometers from Austria. From Lenggries, a hardly used one-lane road goes west along the Alp foothills past sturdy Bayrisch farmhouses, the kind with the barn attached to the house. It's signed to Jachenau, and on to **Wallgau** (see below) and Garmisch.

South of Lenggries is the low **Achen Pass** leading directly to the Inn Tal in Austria and across to the **Ziller Tal** and **Gerlos Pass.**

A large, multi-storied, full-service hotel in Lenggries is the **Brauneck;** D-8172 Lenggries; phone: 080 42-2021. Nearby, a smaller Gasthof is the **Lenggrieser Hof;** D-8172 Lenggries; phone: 080 42-8774.

Closer to Munchen is the **Waldgasthof Buchenhain.** It's in the woods, as its name implies, all by itself. Very Bayerisch in style, it has a beer garden out front. And it has its own train station, so that it's only a few minutes from the city by train, and right on the highway heading for the Alps. D-82065 Baierbrunn/Isar Tal; phone: 89 793-0124; fax: 89 793-8701.

Trip 50   Deutsche Alpenstrasse West

● ●

Distance   *About 110 kilometers from Lindau to Fussen*

Terrain   *Gently sweeping asphalt, one tight climb*

Highlights   *Bucolic countryside, some traffic, photogenic towns, Oberjoch Pass (1180 meters), Balderschwang (1044 meters)*

Lindau is a picturesque island town in Boden See, the very large lake called Lake Constance in English, which is really part of the Rhein River, downstream from all those good passes in Switzerland (see Trips 26, 27) and just west of Bayern. There's a causeway onto Lindau for trains and vehicles. The trains come in frontward, and exit backward, or vice versa. Other vehicles have to park and turn around to leave. The town is all foot traffic. There is marked motorcycle parking.

East from Lindau, the Deutsche Alpenstrasse makes a pleasant sweeping run along the Austrian border. Green meadows and farms. No big mountains.

At Immenstadt a dead-end valley cuts south into the Alps and toward Austria. A part of it, called Klein Walser Tal, actually is in Austria, but you can't get to the rest of Austria from it.

(A small parallel road, just south in Austria, gets to Germany and Immenstadt and the Klein Walser Tal over a pass called **Balderschwang.**)

Heading east, the road climbs up the only really good twisties, the **Oberjoch Pass,** only to run into the Austrian border at 1180 meters elevation. Straight ahead, another small pass, **Gaichtberg** (1093 meters), leads down to Lech Tal and Reutte in Austria. (See Trip 49).

Meanwhile, the Deutsche Alpenstrasse detours north in Germany to Fussen, site of Ludwig's Neuschwanstein castle, where it sort of ends, to resume farther east beyond Garmisch-Partenkirchen.

Hotel Post in Wallgau is a beautiful place to sample Bayerische food as well as architecture. And the road north over Kesselberg isn't bad either.

Trip 51   Deutsche Alpenstrasse East

. . . .

Distance   *About 200 kilometers*

Terrain   *Some rough narrow, some sweeping*

Highlights   *Cute villages (like Wallgau), popular biking roads like
                 Kesselberg (858 meters), Sudelfeld (1097 meters), Ursprung Pass
                 (849 meters), and ★ Rossfeldringstrasse (1536 meters)*

About 12 kilometers east of Garmisch-Partenkirchen on the
road toward Innsbruck, a fork goes north to some interesting
riding and a delightful picture-perfect Bayrisch village, Wallgau. It's close to all the tourists in Garmisch, but hardly
touched by them. Several buildings are elaborately painted,
including the Post Hotel. The inside of the hotel is as interesting as the outside, and so is the food. Locals have *weiss
Wurst,* a sausage made of white meats. Try *Grill Teller,* on
the menu at most Bayrisch and Austrian restaurants. *Grill
Teller* means a plate of grilled meats, usually five or six kinds,
garnished with interesting vegetables.

Before heading on east, a German rider would suggest
going north from Wallgau a few kilometers around a lake,
Walchen See, famous for windsurfing, to climb a little mountain called **Kesselberg.** The tight sweepers of Kesselberg
attract motorcyclists from all of Bayern. So many, in fact, that
the road has been closed to southbound motorcycles on weekends and holidays. There's a rest area turnout on the inside of
a long sweeper that's a *Tofftreffpunkt.* The village of Kochel,
at the north base of Kesselberg, has attractive country hotels.

Back to the Deutsche Alpenstrasse. From the north edge of Wallgau, a tiny, rough, one-lane toll road heads east along the border toward Achen Pass (941 meters). Before it gets to the pass, it becomes a sweeping modern highway.

Once again, straight ahead leads into Austria over little Achen Pass, a wonderful way to get to the Inn Tal below Innsbruck and the Ziller Tal without any traffic. (Into Austria, the Achen Pass road skirts an Alpine lake with many hotels, then makes a sweeping descent into the Inn Tal. A hairpin on the descent, called the Kanzel curve, has a restaurant with a magnificent view of the Inn Tal and the Ziller Tal).

From the Achen Pass, which actually is already in Austria but before the border station, the Deutsche Alpenstrasse goes north again toward a lake, **Tegern See,** which has too much traffic. At Rottach-Egern another bit of one-lane, rough pavement heads south, then north toward another lake with too much traffic, **Schlier See.** (Schlier See is known in history as the site of the "Night of the Long Knives," when, in the mid-thirties, Hitler turned on the brownshirts after they helped him rise to power, and had them killed.) This last leg is sometimes closed to motor traffic which gets detoured north to Schlier See.

East from Schlier See toward **Bayrischzell,** the Alpenstrasse again becomes a modern road—for a while. And from Bayrischzell, another road heads south into Austria and the Inn Tal over another little pass, **Ursprung** (849 meters). Ursprung has two parallel legs descending to Kufstein in the Inn Tal. The southern one is the most fun.

But the best is yet to come: **Sudelfeld.**

East from Bayrischzell, the road climbs and sweeps in a fashion so delightful that it attracts motorcyclists by the hundreds. On weekends, every corner and the little restaurant at the top is full of motorcyclists watching friends sweep back and forth. So much sweeping, in fact, that the local authorities got the road closed to motorcycles. Court cases got it opened again, but with a speed limit.

Funny thing. The great sweeping road just *ends,* or almost does, at a little, narrow toll tunnel that leads down into the Inn Tal. It's possible to turn off east just before the tunnel and head down another narrow, winding road called Tatzelwurm, past a Gasthaus of the same name with a pleasant terrace. Tatzelwurm gets down to the Inn Tal town of **Oberaudorf** on the German side of the Austrian border. Another end of the Deutsche Alpenstrasse.

From Oberaudorf, the best bet is to head straight on east into Austria, over the Inn River (which is the border). About 25 kilometers into Austria, cross back into Germany at **Reit im Winkl,** a village with many cute buildings decorated in Bavarian style. Here the Deutsche Alpenstrasse takes off again in good sweeping style toward Berchtesgaden. (South of Reit im Winkl, a wide, smooth Austrian road winds easily through mountains to Lofer and the roads of Trip 48.) Berchtesgaden is touristy.

On the mountain above Berchtesgaden is the best part of the whole Deutsche Alpenstrasse, the **Rossfeldringstrasse.** This trip (about 25 km) is high dancing along the Austrian border, with gorgeous views across Salzburg and its valley to the high Tannengebirge mountains in Austria and in the other direction, over Berchtesgaden. There are several restaurants on the ring road. To get up on the ring from Berchtesgaden, follow the signs to Obersalzberg, a steep climb in the direction of Hitler's Eagles Nest. The Rossfeldringstrasse turns off, and then there's a toll booth! In fact, there are two toll booths, one at each end of the toll part of the ring road.

From the ring road there's a well-kept secret way down into Austria with easy access to the Austrian Autobahn. It's pretty and fun and hardly ever used by anyone. Just below the northerly toll booth, a small road heads north. That's it. It has no significant marking, but it goes to a tiny border crossing, and then down to the Austrian mountain town, Durrnberg, site of the famous Salzburg salt mines, then on down to come out in the valley of the Salzach River at the Austrian village of Hallein. It's much easier to get to the Rossfeldringstrasse on this road from **Hallein,** just south of Salzburg, than from Germany through Berchtesgaden. From Hallein, Austria, look for the new bridge looping over the main street and up the mountainside just north of the old town. The new bridge is the road. (See Trip 55).

Hordes of tourists visit the salt mines at Durrnberg, but they come up a little cable car from Hallein, not the road.

Austria East of the Tirol

Central Austria south of Salzburg is the very narrow waist of the country, just over 100 kilometers across, from Berchtesgaden in Germany to Italy. Innsbruck, Tirol, and Vorarlberg are in the west, and Wien (Vienna) is to the east. Since the narrow waist area is all high mountains with many good north-south pass roads, there's a lot of good riding.

There are millions of Germans on one side and millions of Italians on the other side of Austria's narrow waist, all busy going back and forth across little Austria, such a short distance across that they need not stop for even a WC, let alone gas. Except that prudent Austria has concluded that most of this north-south traffic should pay a toll. A couple of the roads are actually private enterprise endeavors.

Austrian private enterprise has also provided a plethora of tourist accommodations. In the first two trips described here, there's a Gasthaus on practically every corner, with Zimmer Freis in between. Most hotels are attractive Austrian mountain style, with huge roofs, balconies garlanded with flower boxes, and interesting illustrations painted on exterior walls. They almost guarantee good food, attentive service, and spotless, attractive accommodations. Many have elaborate carved wood and wrought iron detailing. There are so many establishments, all so inviting, that any traveler with an economic bent must wonder how they can possibly produce a return on what has to be a very large investment. To an American mind they just don't make economic sense, but they surely are nice.

Most of the hotels spend as much on cooking as on decoration. Area sweet specialties besides *Apfel Strudel* include *Toffel Strudel* (more of a custard base), both with vanilla sauce or the more standard whipped cream. *Kaiser Schmarrn* is a crepe-like concoction smothered in fruit. Practically every menu will have a *Grill Teller,* or mixed grill platter. Sometimes it's good to ask for recommendations. Find out what is just out of the oven, or is specially prepared.

The **Hotel Glocknerhof** is spectacularly set in the high mountain village of **Heiligenblut** on the south side of the Grossglockner. It hangs on the mountain edge at the entrance to the village with views of the very Austrian village church (tall steeple) and craggy mountains across the green *Moll Tal* (valley) below. Even the indoor swimming pool has sweeping mountain views. The interior is spacious and charming modern mountain design. A-9844 Heiligenblut; phone: 048 24-2244.

Four hotels in central Austria advertise themselves as MoHo, Motorrad Hotels in the Alps. They specialize in serving motorcyclists. Each is different. They are completely adequate and moderately priced. You can be sure that some part of the family running each is a motorcycle enthusiast, and that all involved will speak motorcycle.

Landhaus Jausern; A-5753 Saalbach; phone: 065 41-7341. It's high in a dead-end valley just north of **Zell am See** and south of Salzburg. From the main road into Saalbach, turn south. Landhaus Jausern is behind and above a larger hotel.

Hotel Iselsbergerhof; A-9991 Iselsberg; phone: 048 526-4112; fax: 048 526-41124. It's on the low pass road of the same name south of the Grossglockner and just north of Lienz.

One of the MoHo's, Hotel Solaria, is a good choice for trips in the next chapter, Salzburg Land, where it's listed. Another is north of Innsbruck, so it's listed with Trip 48.

Trip 52 Achen Pass and the Ziller Tal

....

Distance   About 170 kilometers from Germany via Zillertaler Hohenstrasse,
                 Schlegeis, Gerlos Pass, to Grossglockner

Terrain   Good sweepers, narrow erratic road on Zillertaler Hohenstrasse,
                 old Gerlos

Highlights   Lovely farms and villages, fun roads with some traffic spots, good
                 hotels and cafes. Includes: Achen Pass (941 meters), Zillertaler
                 Hohenstrasse, Schlegeis (1784 meters), Gerlos Pass (1507
                 meters), Konigsleiten, Pass Thurn (1273 meters)

The Achen Pass (see Trip 51, Deutsche Alpenstrasse) sweeps
magnificently down into the Inn Tal, and it's possible to
proceed across the autobahn and right up the Ziller Tal, a
valley with every imaginable shade of green. The Ziller Tal
is decorated with a narrow gauge railroad, sometimes sporting a chuffing steam-powered train. At **Zell am Ziller,** the
Gerlos Pass road leaves the Ziller Tal and starts climbing a
finger valley to the east.

But before that, at Ried, the **Zillertaler Hohenstrasse**
climbs the mountainside to the west, where it hangs and
dances in a one-lane game in and out of the tree line, offering
dazzling views of the yellow-green, blue-green, and green-
green quilt below and the Gerlos Pass road snaking up opposite. It finally comes back down in the Ziller Tal at Ramsberg.
There's a toll.

Atop the Zillertaler Hohenstrasse is the Almgasthof
Zirmstadl of interesting log construction and sporting a terrace with a fine view.

Head farther south up the Ziller Tal past Mayrhofen and
Finkenberg. Just above Finkenberg, traffic is directed to a
new road and tunnel going farther up the valley. The old road,
to the right, is the correct choice. It snakes through a gorge
with overhanging cliffs. Snuggled against the cliffs is the
Gasthaus Jodburg; A-6292 Finkenberg 595; phone: 052
851-8110. Another hotel is Sporthotel Stock; A-6292
Finkenberg; phone: 052 85-6775; fax: 052 85-677-5421.

Farther up, a toll road with a one-way-at-a-time traffic light leads into the high **Schlegeis.** Near the end of the road, a gravel drive leads up above a lake to the Dominikushutte, a restaurant with a view of Italian mountain peaks. It's a good turnaround spot.

Back down at Zell am Ziller, the Gerlos climbs east through a tourist town of the same name, **Gerlos.** Near the top there's a toll gate onto a new swooping alignment that supposedly offers views of the Krimmler waterfall. The views are from quite a distance. Turn north and take the old road instead. It bounces and weaves and heaves in great sport down the mountain. Part is narrow. Some bridges are wooden. There may be signs advising (in German, of course) that on some days and at some hours, work may be in progress. Bikes can probably get through even if work is in progress. Certainly Gasthaus operators on the old road will hope so!

Near the top of the Gerlos, just about where the toll road splits off, is an opportunity to climb a bit higher to a ski village called **Konigsleiten,** with a couple of good hotels. **Hotel Gasthof Ursprung;** A-5742 Konigsleiten; Wald-Pinzgau; phone: 065 648-253-8271; fax: 065 648-2538.

From the Gerlos, it's straight ahead east to Zell am See and the Grossglockner, skirting the high Tauern mountain spine of Austria to the south, and the Kitzbuhel Alps to the north. At **Mittersill,** little **Pass Thurn** joins from the north, and the

Four hotels in Austria advertise themselves as MoHo, Motorcycle Hotels. Hotel Solaria, high atop the Obertauern Pass, and set back from the main road, is easy for a biker to find.

big **Felbertauern toll tunnel** road joins from the south, coming out from under the Hohe Tauern mountains. The Felbertauern tunnel is the main north-south, all-weather connection across the waist of Austria, parallel to the Grossglockner.

The narrow old road above Mayrhofen up to Schlegeis hugs the cliffs under overhanging rocks.

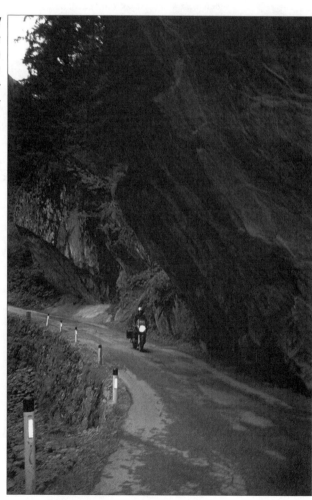

Trip 53   Passes From Italy

Distance   *From Italy to Grossgiockner, via Staller Sattel, about 65 kilometers; via Plocken Pass, about 50 kilometers; via Nassfeld Pass, about 60 kilometers*

Terrain   *Via Staller Sattel, good sweepers; via Plocken Pass, pleasant road; via Nassfeld Pass, pleasant road*

Highlights   *Via ★ Staller Sattel (2052 meters), pretty country, hotels in east Tirol; via Plocken Pass (1362 meters), quick connection over Gailberg Sattel (982) to Grossglockner; via Nassfeld Pass (1557 meters), good escape from Italian autostrada; ★ Kartischer Sattel (1526 meters)*

Staller Sattel is the fun one-way-at-a-time pass into Austria from the Dolomites in Italy (see Trip 44). It comes down into Austria from the one-way part, past the Tan-dlerstub'n hotel restaurant in St. Jakob, joining the Felber-tauern road south of the tunnel, and goes on into the major city of the Ost (east) Tirol, **Lienz.** (The Ost Tirol is the part that voted to rejoin Austria in the 1920s after it had been awarded to Italy at Versailles. It is separated from the rest of the Austrian Tirol by the Sud Tirol, still part of Italy.)

From Lienz, a fine sweeper climbs the **Iselsberg Pass** (site of one of the motorcycle hotels) toward Heiligenblut and the Grossglockner. The Iselsberg provides the last (or first) glimpses of the Dolomites.

East of the Dolomites, east of Cortina d'Ampezzo, two seldom-used passes—Plocken and Nassfeld—cross from Italy into Austria (they aren't usually called by their Italian names, Passo di Monte Croce Carnico and Passo di Pramollo). (See Trip 44.)

The Plocken especially has an exciting climb up out of Italy in layered switchbacks through forests. The Nassfeld is just ten kilometers off the autostrada/Autobahn between Venezia and Wien. It's a wonderful way to escape the diesel trucks and buses of the autostrada. Both passes enter a seldom-traversed Austrian valley of pleasant interest. From it, the Gailberg Sattel connects directly to Lienz in the East Tirol, Iselsberg, and the Grossglockner. Right where the Gailberg Sattel connects, at Kotschach-Mauthen, is one of the MoHos, the **Gailtaler Hof;** phone: 047 15-318; fax: 047 15-8787.

West from the Gailtaler Hof at Kotschach is a gnarly, tight, twisty road up the Lesach Tal to **Kartischer Sattel** (1526 meters) leading to the East Tirol near the Italian border. (The road actually starts at the hotel.)

The Plocken Pass makes an audacious climb out of Italy into Austria, leading toward the Grossglockner.

Trip 54 Grossglockner

Distance	*About 200 kilometers over Grossglockner to Salzburg*
Terrain	*Every kind of mountain road: tight, sweeping, narrow hairpins over a major pass and a couple of lesser ones*
Highlights	*Exhilarating riding and scenery. Includes:* ★*Grossglockner Hoch Tor (2575 meters), Edelweiss Spitze (2577 meters),* ★*Grossglockner Fuscher Tor (2428 meters), Filzen Sattel (1291 meters), Dientener Sattel (1357 meters)*

The Grossglockner Hochalpenstrasse, Grossglockner for short, is one of the major play roads of the Alps. In crossing the highest spine of the Austrian Alps, it combines every test of driving skill: hairpins, sweepers, jig-jags, cobblestones, steep descents, narrow ledges, sometimes ice and snow and hanging clouds of fog, along with spectacular views and plenty of restaurants. It's only a half-day's drive from Munchen and the big cities of northern Italy, and even less from Salzburg, so it is a testing spot for the latest machines and visiting drivers. And it's private enterprise.

Yes, it's a private toll road. And fairly expensive. Typically, the Austrians in cute costumes at the toll booths will take any kind of money. Once through the toll booths, it's possible to play back and forth and up and down to the heart's content, even stay at one of the several hotels. If a return trip is anticipated from outside the toll booths, it's possible to arrange a slightly reduced price in advance. Environmentalists are raising some Cain about limiting access to the Grossglockner Hochalpenstrasse—too many tourists tramping about looking for Edelweiss—but private enterprise and the profit motive have kept it open so far. (Sorry, Austrians don't know the popular song, "Edelweiss," from *The Sound of Music*.)

The south half of the Grossglockner is in the state of Karnten, which we English speakers call Carinthia. The north part of the Grossglocker is in Salzburg Land.

The approach from the north is up the Fuscher Tal, a lush green valley, from Zell am See and Bruck, past the village of **Fusch.** Then the climb.

There are two short tunnels and two humps across the top. The north hump is called **Fuscher Tor** (Fusch Gate) and the other **Hoch** (high) **Tor,** with a high Alpine valley between the two, where the road often cuts through deep snow banks.

Near the Fuscher Tor, what looks like a restaurant parking lot leads to the snaking little road up to the highest point, **Edelweiss Spitze.** The road's worth the trip. The view from the restaurant at the top is reward enough. The restaurant, Edelweiss Hutte, is down over the edge from the parking lot.

From Edelweiss Spitze on the Grossglockner, the pass road is a ribbon across high Alpine valleys, disappearing into tunnels (left) and dropping off the edge to the north.

Sometimes it's possible to ride down to it. Above, all around are high peaks, and below, bits of ribbon roads. To the south, the ribbon, not really a ribbon but a string, works across the Alpine meadows. Until August it's just a slit in deep snow banks that disappears into a tunnel. To the north, the road seems to weave to the mountain's edge and then disappear into the Fuscher Tal.

Time for hot chocolate.

About halfway down the south side, well below the Hoch Tor, a road leads about nine kilometers around the mountain to a huge parking garage called Franz Josefs Hohe. There's a view of the Grossglockner itself, the big mountain that's supposed to look like a big bell, and a cable car ride down onto the ice of the Pasterze Glacier. Bikes can usually find a nook or cranny or a piece of sidewalk to park on outside the huge garage. Some of the road to the garage and back is in concrete snow sheds.

Just outside the southern toll booths is the high village of Heiligenblut (Holy Blood), whose name sounds better untranslated. Besides the Glocknerhof, there are several other hotels and Gasthaus possibilities. There's often an evening brass band concert in the little town square, backed by a fountain made of huge mountain crystals. The little church at Heiligenblut is a good example of the original Austrian Gothic that has not been baroqued. The memorials in it illustrate the horrible costs of 20th century wars to families of the village.

South from Heiligenblut, down the Moll Tal, is the Iselsberg Pass (site of one of the MoHos) up and over toward Lienz and the Dolomites of Italy, the passes of Trip 53. North of the Grossglockner, and north of Zell am See about five kilometers, is the turnoff to Saalbach, site of another MoHo. A few kilometers farther north is **Saalfelden** and the pleasant Austrian roads to Reit im Winkl on the Deutsche Alpenstrasse.

A new tunnel through the adjacent mountain eases the traffic around Zell am See. But a better route is to head around the east side of the See (Zell's on the west), then continue on country lanes through Gerling to Maria Alm.

The main road north from Zell am See goes to **Saalfelden,** then heads east to Maria Alm, a pleasant village pleasantly bypassed by the new road up the **Filzen Sattel.** Beyond Maria Alm, the Sattel road climbs steeply and irregularly. Parts have been improved, but the old sections are the most fun. All of this is just south of Berchtesgaden and the Rossfeldringstrasse in Germany.

The road dips, then climbs the **Dientener Sattel.**

The countryside is rural, remote and tourist free all the way across the Sattels and down a twisting gorge to Bischofshofen. The road bypasses most of Bischofshofen, connecting straight across the Salzach River to the Tauern Autobahn high on the mountain opposite. The Autobahn connects Salzburg with southern Austria and Italy. It's free except for a toll tunnel through the highest part of the Tauern mountains.

Take the Autobahn about ten kilometers south to the Lammer Tal exit, and follow the Tal north on the Salzburger Dolomitenstrasse along a raging mountain stream through Annaberg to Abtenau, sweeping down to the Salzach at **Golling.** Might as well take the Autobahn to Salzburg.

It's only six more hairpins like this from Fuscher Tor on the Grossglockner to Edelweiss Spitze.

SEE
"DEUTSCHE ALPEN-
STRASSE" Trips 50-51

Autobahn

Gmunden

Micheldorf

Salzburgring

Mond See

Traun See

Alm Tal

SALZBURG

Wolfgang See

Bad Ischl

Pyrn Pass

Hallein

Strobl

Rossfeldringstrasse

Post Alm

Potschen Hohe

Liezen

Germany

Golling

Abtenau

Pass Gschutt

Stein a.d. Enns

Filzmoos

Eben

Radstadt

Ramsau

Solker Pass

SEE "AUSTRIA
EAST OF THE TIROL"
TRIPS 52-54

Radstadter Tauern Pass

Schoder

0   5   10 15 20 25
km

Mauterndorf

Tamsweg

Seetaler

Murau

SEE
"KARNTEN LAND"
TRIPS 58-60

Salzburg Land

EASTERN PART OF SALZBURG LAND

Kalte Kuchl

Mariazell

(Lahn Sattel

Pyrn Pass

Aflenzer Seeberg)(

Gesause

Admont

Eisenerz

)(Prabichl Pass

Aflenz-Kurort

)(Rottenmanner Pass

Leoben

Osterreichring

Judenberg

)(Gaberl Sattel

0 5 10 15 20 25
km

Austria

Salzburg is the name of a state, Salzburg Land, as well as of the city.

Bookshelves are full of stuff about the romance of Salzburg, the city, what with Mozart and the *Sound of Music.* But are there many about the entertaining roads around it?

And there's an easy-to-get-to hotel, out on the fringe of congestion that's motorcycle friendly. (And it got its beer license several hundred years ago.). **Gasthof Brauwirt;** A-5101 Lengfelden; phone: 066 245-4128; fax: 066 245-412853. Find it by going a couple of kilometers north from the Salzburg Nord Autobahn Ausfahrt (Salzburg North exit). The hotel is off the road on the west side.

One of the MoHos, the motorcycle hotels, is in Salzburg Land atop **Radstadter Tauern Pass. Hotel Solaria;** A-5562 Obertauern; phone: 064 56-7250; fax: 064 56-7549. Balconies have views of snowy slopes. The turn is marked by a brightly painted old motorcycle for a sign. The hotel has recently been completely renovated.

Trip 55   Post Alm

....

Distance	*165 kilometers*
Terrain	*Narrow mountain roads and pretty country*
Highlights	*Salzkammergut lakes, Post Alm (about 1500 meters) (toll), Gaisberg (1287 meters) bucolic mountains and views*

Take the Autobahn in the direction of Wien, east, for about twenty-five kilometers, exiting at **Mond See.** This is the Salzkammergut, land of lakes and mountains. South along some lakes, and over a low pass brings you to St. Gilgen on **St. Wolfgang See.** Mozart's mother lived here. The main road east from St. Gilgen follows the south shore of the lake as far as **Strobl,** where a mini-interchange has a sign pointing south to **Post Alm.** It's a little road that climbs through the forest with some switchbacks. No tourists. There's a toll.

Near the top, the through road turns sharply left, signed for "**Abtenau.**" Straight ahead goes to a parking lot for hikers. Climbing up over another hump, a Gasthof can be spotted on the mountainside with a little drive leading up to it, **Gasthof Alpenrose;** A-53050 Strobl; phone and fax: 061 37-6111.

After wandering down into a lovely valley, the Post Alm road gets to a tee-intersection. Turning east is a real adventure. It seems like driving through farm driveways. But it connects with the main road back through Abtenau and down to Golling.

North of Golling, at Hallein, detour up the Durrnberg road to the Rossfeldringstrasse, if you haven't done it (Trip 51). It affords great views of Salzburg, Golling, and the mountains of this trip.

From Hallein, a road heads northeast, behind Salzburg, coming out east of the city right at the **Salzburgring,** the famous G.P. race track. Back toward Salzburg five miles, a road climbs Gaisberg mountain. From it, Salzburg is all spread out below.

Trip 56   Filzmoos and Tauern Passes

Distance	*130 kilometers, plus a turn on the Autobahn*
Terrain	*Back and forth on the Tauern mountains, some small roads, steep climbs and switchbacks*
Highlights	*Filzmoos (1056 meters), Ramsau (1135 meters), Solker Tauern Pass (1788 meters), Radstadter Tauern Pass (1739 meters), Seetaler Sattel (1246 meters)*

★

Hotel Solaria, one of the MoHos listed at the head of the chapter, Salzburg Land, is atop the Radstadter Tauern Pass on this trip.

Two rivers run roughly parallel, from west to east, south of Salzburg, the Enns and the Mur with the Tauern mountains in between. This route crosses the Tauern mountains from one valley to the next, and then back. Trip 58, Turracher and Nockalm, adjoins this trip on the south.

South of Salzburg, on the Tauern Autobahn, exit at the **Eben** Ausfahrt, just past the Gasthofgut, and head east up the mountain road to **Filzmoos,** an attractive mountain village with lots of hotels and restaurants. East of Filzmoos, toward **Ramsau,** the road becomes much less traveled. Keep east and the road eventually comes down in the valley of the Enns River, the Enns Tal. There'll be signs to **Stein a.d. Enns,** across on the south side of the river. That's the gateway to **Solker Pass,** a non-commercial north-south crossing of the Tauern mountains. It's a good road, decorated by many signs, each the silhouette of a motorcycle with the words "slowly" in many languages, including English. But it's a great climb. On the north side, short of the top, is a gravel driveway leading to a very comfortable restaurant, the Erzherzog Johann Hutte. At the top of the pass is a big sign in German addressed to "Dear Motorcycle Riders" and saying in effect that if you don't watch your playful speed on this road, maybe, and then there's the symbol of "motorcycles forbidden." It's a good ride anyway. The south side is through mostly unoccupied forests.

From **Schoder** at the south base of the Solker, head west on very lightly traveled roads high above the Mur Tal, playing along the south edges of the Tauern mountains through Krakaudorf, over **Seetaler Sattel,** and on west to **Tamsweg,** a fair sized town, and on to **Mauterndorf.** At 1122 meters, with a photo-worthy castle, Mauterndorf is the gateway back

Almost at the gates of Wein, the most easterly passes of the Alps attract motorcyclists from the city. The Gasthaus at Kalte Kuchl is right where a couple of good roads intersect.

north over the Radstadter Tauern Pass to Salzburg. The pass road climbs through high meadowlands, then rather steeply to the top of the pass at the village, **Obertauern,** site of the MoHo Solaria. (Look for the motorcycle beside the road.)

A short way down the north side of the pass there's a small monument which recognizes the work of Russian prisoners who built the road during World War I. (Austria was pretty successful in its eastern front battles with Russia in that war. Of course, the Russian revolution started. Meanwhile, the serfs built this road for us to enjoy.) Below the monument, the road enters a narrow gorge and twists beside a rushing stream before daylighting in some rolling hills with quaint farmhouses leading to the town Radstadt and the Autobahn back to Salzburg.

Trip 57   Near Vienna

Distance	*About 300 kilometers from Salzburg to Aflenz-Kurort*
Terrain	*Gently sweeping over low passes*
Highlights	*Popular, scenic lakes and lower mountains, occasional narrow roads, popular motorcycle cafe at Kalte Kuchl. Includes: Pass Gschutt (969 meters), Potschen Hohe (992 meters), Aflenzer Seeberg (1253 meters), Rottenmanner Hohentauern (1278 meters), Lahn Sattel (1015 meters), Kalte Kuchl, Gaberl Sattel (1547 meters)*

Motorradhotel Hubertushof is almost at the eastern terminus of this trip, just south of **Mariazell,** just north of Bruck an der Mur, and not too far west of Wien. It's at Mariazellerstrasse 45; A-8623 Aflenz-Kurort; phone: 038 61-3131. The owner is a dealer for several brands of bikes. Kurort roughly translates as spa, or cure, village. So **Aflenz-Kurort** is an attractive village nestled in alpine foothills, bypassed by main highways, with public baths and pools. It's hardly ever seen an American.

East of Salzburg and east of the Solker Pass, almost as far as Wien, are lovely lakes and low mountains that have cap-

tured the hearts of romanticists. Names like Salzkammergut,
St. Wolfgang See, **Bad Ischl** (a favorite of Kaiser Franz
Joseph up to World War I), **Gesause,** Mariazell and Raxalpe
are famous. Some roads are nice. Some, not so nice. Nothing
is exotic. Nothing is like the Dolomites or Andermatt or the
Grossglockner. Some of the valleys are rather tedious and
industrial.

South of Salzburg on the Autobahn, past Hallein where
the road climbs up to the Rossfeldringstrasse, at the Golling
Ausfahrt, a wonderfully pleasant sweeping road heads up and
east through a fine mountain village, Abtenau, and on across
low **Pass Gschutt,** to a popular mountain lake, Halstatter See.
Almost the whole thing is new, sweeping, smooth asphalt.
North around the Halstatter See leads to another lowly
pass, **Potschen Hohe** and to Bad Aussee. South around
Halstatter See is a smaller road that takes a tunnel around a
village, then makes a steep rough climb to Bad Aussee.

Bad Ischl and St. Wolfgang See are north of this route on
the main road east from Salzburg. North of Bad Ischl are
some nice roads climbing small passes between lovely lakes.
There's one between Bad Ischl and Attersee, and one between Attersee and **Gmunden,** and one between Gmunden
and **Micheldorf.** Midway on the latter is Scharnstein. South
from Scharnstein, an interesting dead-end road up the **Alm
Tal** leads to a tight, twisting climb through the woods on a
one-lane paved road to a high restaurant-hotel called the
Hochberghaus; A-4645 Grunau im Alm Tal-Salzkammer-
gut; phone: 076 16-8477. The road up is called the
Bergstrasse Farrenau.

The main road south from Micheldorf climbs over the low
Pyhrn Pass (954 meters) to the Gesause region at **Admont.**
A quick climb over a little path straight south from Admont
connects in sixteen kilometers to Trieben and the **Rottenmanner Hohentauern** pass road, and immediately south of
that through **Judenburg** is the **Gaberl Sattel** toward Graz.
The Osterreichring race track is just northeast of Judenburg.

Meanwhile, the Gesause road, east from Admont, is rather
uneventful, although famous. It runs east toward the
Prabichl Pass at **Eisenerz.** The countryside looks like it has
been strip mined, and Eisenerz looks like a "company town"

in Wales or West Virginia. Steyr, home of Puch, is down-stream from Eisenerz, and the Prabichl, the source of its iron ore.

The Alps have their last fling about 90 kilometers short of Wien. The area is easily reached from the Motorradhotel Hubertushof at Aflenz-Kurort, listed above. The *Tofftref-fpunkt,* for riders of Wien and eastern Austria, who know where the nearby good roads are, is an intersection with a Gasthof called **Kalte Kuchl.** Despite its name ("cold kitchen"), it has good hot food, and the terraces are full of bikers on weekends. The two passes of note, **Lahn Sattel** and **Aflenzer Seeberg,** are between Aflenz-Kurort and Kalte Kuchl.

Karnten Land

Austria's southern state Karnten, that we call Carinthia, borders both Italy and Slovenia. Slovenia is that northern part of former Yugoslavia that ajoins Italy. Karnten is a land of mountains and lakes, which some have called warmer than the rest of Austria. Routes of Trip 56 are to the north, and routes of Trip 44 are southwest of it.

Two possible hotels illustrate the area's variety.

One is in **Villach,** a medium size town in the valley of the Drau River that flows out of the Dolomites of Italy and across southern Austria into Slovenia.

Almost next door to the cathedral, the Dom, in Villach, is the **Hotel Post.** Another Hotel Post. Hauptplatz 26; A-9500 Villach; phone: 042 422-61010; fax: 042 422-610-1420. The Hauptplatz is a walking zone, so it's necessary to ride in to the hotel's courtyard from the back.

A road west right out of the middle of Villach climbs in a couple of kilometers to almost 1000 meters at Bad Bleiberg.

About thirty kilometers north of Villach is the mountain village **Bad Kleinkirchheim** with several hotels capitalizing on the mountains and the water. **Hotel Pulverer;** A-9546 Bad Kleinkirchheim; phone: 042 40-744; fax: 042 4-0793. It's pretty fancy with many pools inside and out and water slides and huge jacuzzi baths and very good food.

Trip 58   Turracher and Nockalm

Distance	*200 Kilometers*
Terrain	*Seldom traveled mountain roads and passes, some narrow*
Highlights	*Flattnitz (1400 meters), Turracher Hohe (1783 meters), Nockalmstrasse (toll) with Eisen Tal Hohe (2042 meters) and Heiligenbach (1920 meters), Dr. Josef Mehrl Hutte (1700 meters), Katchberg Pass (1641 meters), Porsche Museum*

The Mur River and the Drau River are roughly parallel, flowing from west to east. This route weaves back and forth several times across the mountain that separates them.

The south part of Trip 56 was across the Mur north of this trip.

Northeast of Villach, and east of Bad Kleinkirchheim is a village **Kleinglodnitz** where a scenic road climbs north up a valley to **Flattnitz,** and wends down to the Mur. You know when you get there because there's a railroad track beside the Mur. Cross the tracks and only six kilometers west is **Predlitz** where the **Turracher Hohe** road heads back south across the mountain. The climb is sweeping and fun to the top where there are several restaurants and hotels. The descent on the south side is very steep, a 23% grade, so if it's cold on top, you can warm up fast.

As soon as the road flattens out, there's an intersection with the **Nockalmstrasse,** marked by a cute waterwheel. It's a sharp turn, back northwesterly across the mountain again. Like on the Grossglockner, there's a toll on the Nockalm, and like on the Grossglockner, there are restaurants and small hotels and you can play back and forth before exiting. There are two high points on the road, which finally makes it down to the valley of the Kremsbach, at a village called **Innerkrems.** The other Krems is downstream. But don't go that way. Turn easterly, upstream on a road that doesn't look very promising. But it crosses the next mountain at a place identified only as **Dr. Josef Mehrl Hutte,** and comes down in the Mur side of the mountain in a tee-intersection. Head west through **Pichlern** and in six kilometers join the main highway crossing back south over the **Katchberg Pass.** The Katchberg is rather steep on both sides. And all of a sudden there is traffic, because the Katchberg parallels the Tauern Autobahn from Salzburg, and at this point, the autobahn has a toll. The Katchberg doesn't.

South of the Katchberg, you'll be amazed at the towering concrete structures far overhead, carrying the Autobahn down the narrow valley without scarring the mountains, leaving farms and villages underneath it. There is an Autobahn connection just at the base of the Katchberg, and there's no toll to go on south. The entrance to the Autobahn is called Rennweg . . . raceway. On either road, up on the Autobahn or down below on the regular road, head south to **Gmund,** site of the famous Porsche Museum. It's necessary to loop into and around the village of Gmund to get to the museum. Many collector cars are on display.

Villach, the Drau, and Bad Kleinkirchheim are farther down south.

Trip 59   Klippitztorl

Distance	*240 Kilometers, some Autobahn*
Terrain	*Narrow roads, Klippitztorl (1644 meters), Weinebene (1668 meters), Hebalpe (1360 meters)*
Highlights	*Exploring non-tourist, rural Austria*

North and east of Villach and Bad Kleinkirchheim is **Althofen.** It's north of Karnten's capital city, **Klagenfurt.** East of Althofen about seven kilometers is **Mosel,** and just north of Mosel, the **Klippitztorl** road climbs east over the mountains, wending to 1644 meters. Not much of anybody there but there is a restaurant hut near the top that may be surprised to see you.

Down east in the next valley, head south about thirteen kilometers crossing under the Autobahn to **St. Gertraud,** where another nobody's-on-it road into the mountains in a southeasterly direction crosses over **Weinebene.** In about 35 kilometers it comes down in a pretty good sized town, **Deutschlandsberg.** In the town there are signs for **St. Oswald** and **Hebalpe,** in a northwesterly direction. The route is very pleasant, crossing over the mountains to an Autobahn, one that connects Graz and Wien to the northeast with Karnten, to the southwest. Take it.

Trip 60   Three Country Loop

• •

Distance	*200 kilometers*
Terrain	*Modestly high passes, narrow roads*
Highlights	*Loop across Wurzen Pass (1073 meters) into Slovenia, through Triglavski Narodni, Slovenia's National Park, Vrsic Pass (1611 meters) World War I fort and monument, Passo de Predil (1150 meters) into Italy, Passo Sella Nevea (1190 meters), Nassfeld Pass (1557 meters) into Austria, Windische Hohe (1110 meters) Kreuzberg Sattel (1077 meters), Gailberg Sattel (982 meters)*

Villach is just north of where Slovenia (formerly part of Yugoslavia) borders Italy. This loop south from Villach explores that three country corner.

Wurzen Pass into Slovenia is signed, straight up and south from Villach. It's only fifteen kilometers from downtown to the border at the top of the pass.

Insurance for vehicles registered in Europe should be valid in Slovenia, which many consider the most stable of the new republics. Check the green card to be sure SLO, Slovenia, is not crossed out. It probably is crossed out on most vehicles not registered in Europe. If it is crossed out, it will be necessary to buy Slovenian insurance at the border. It's not a bargain. It might be handy to get Slovenian money, too.

Just down off the pass into Slovenia a few kilometers, there's a junction. Jog easterly a couple of kilometers and turn south by **Kranjska Gora** to climb southerly up the **Vrsic Pass.** It's a good road, and the reason is apparent after a few switchbacks. There's a very Russian looking church in the woods. It is Russian. It was built by Russian prisoners during World War I while they were working on the road. This is the National Park, Triglavski Narodni, that occupies a large part of northwestern Slovenia.

There's a modest restaurant at the top of the pass, and a good sweeping road down in a southwesterly direction. At the junction at the bottom, head northerly, back up the **Passo de Predil.** In World War I, this area was all in Austria and the Predil was the border with the Italian enemy. So near the top of the pass is a stone fort much like those in the Dolomites. It's sited to command the valley approaches. There are metal rungs in the cliff opposite the fort, apparently installed like a ladder to some higher observation point. It looks pretty exposed. Nearby, in an arcing curve of the road, is an elaborate monument honoring an Austrian nobleman who apparently came to grief in the area.

Across the border, it's only a couple of kilometers down to an intersection. The road southeast is a pleasant and forgotten pass, the **Passo Sella Nevea,** with an Italian ristorante.

The Italian road wanders west through relatively unoccupied mountains, and then meets the main autostrada connecting this part of Italy with Austria. Take it or the regular road beside it north only eight kilometers to **Pontebba.** Cross the bridge, leaving the autostrada to head east. Go straight north. Actually, not very straight, very twistily. It's only thirteen kilometers up to the Austrian border and the **Nassfeld Pass** (Passo di Promollo in Italian). It's just twelve kilometers down the pass. Head east seven kilometers to **Hermagor.**

Or get to Hermagor the long way, by heading west to **Kotschach,** north over the Gailberg Sattel, and east from **Oberdrauberg** to **Greifenburg,** then up the **Kreuzberg Sattel** to Hermagor. Just about 100 kilometers extra.

From Hermagor, head easterly to **Tratten,** and climb north over the **Windische Hohe,** down to the valley of the **Drau** and Villach.

Corsica

▲ Corsica

• •

Corsica should be on every motorcyclist's must-do list.

Little more than 150 kilometers, north to south, and 80 kilometers wide, it's packed with high rugged mountains—even some skiing—and gorges and canyons and passes with enough tight, twisty roads to exhaust the most ardent enthusiast. It takes a week of all-day riding to cover the roads.

And it's breathtakingly gorgeous. Exotic rock formations in all colors, rushing streams and waterfalls, pine forests, chestnut forests, deserts, and cliffs down to private little beaches.

Because most Americans might have difficulty finding Corsica on the map (and because most Corsicans have never seen an American) here's a bit about it.

It's an island in the Mediterranean south of **Genova,** west of **Livorno** (and Pisa), and north of **Sardinia** (Sardegna in Italian). For 200 years it's been French. For a thousand before that it was Italian, under Genova or Pisa, with a bit of Spain thrown in. To Italians it was Corsica. That's what we call it. Germans use "k"s, Korsika. But in French, it's Corse, or le Corse. There's Italian food and French food. But the money,

On Corsica, roads like the Scala de Santa Regina lead from mountain tops to quiet sandy beaches.

the stamps, the phone, and the police are all French. Le Corse is a department of metropolitan France. And there's the rub. Some locals would rather not be.

The difference need not affect motorcyclists. Surely not the thousands of bikers that fill most every ferry to and from the island. The ferries to Corsica often look like those to the Isle of Man during TT time, packed with every kind of motorcycle imaginable. There's play room for all.

You don't have to worry too much about high brow culture on Corsica. Some prehistoric types—like 20,000 years ago—carved figures on the southwest coast. The Romans tried unsuccessfully to farm the few level parts on the east coast. Since then various city states and kings fought with scant success to control the island. There were lots of places to hide in those mountains and canyons that we love today.

Several coastal towns, notably **Calvi** on the northwest coast and **Bonifacio** on the south tip, remain walled fortresses left over from the battles of the Middle Ages. Then there's the fortress of independent Corsica in the middle of the mountains at **Corte.**

The proud symbol of Corsica is a black head with a white headband.

There are only a couple of kilometers of more or less straight road, just south of **Bastia** on the northeast coast. The main road across the island and mountains from Bastia to **Ajaccio** on the opposite coast swoops and sweeps in daringly inviting asphalt—and the locals dare—to 1163 meters at the **Col de Vizzavona.** Most other roads are so gnarly and/or so precipitous as to require constant attention while providing exciting riding pleasures. They climb through such wild landscapes that it seems you're exploring some strange planet, not a small European island. Ride in the mountains all day. Sleep by the seashore.

Tourist offices: Offices de Tourisme; 1 Place Foch; F-21076 Ajaccio; phone: 495 21-4087.

Offices de Tourisme de la Haute; Corse; F-20200 Bastia; phone: 495 31-0204.

How to Get There

Fly. Sail. Bikers will probably ferry to Corsica from the continent. There are multiple ways.

Three companies do most of the ferrying. One French. Two Italian.

The French one, SNCM Ferryterranee, sails from French ports like Marseille and Nice and Toulon. The Italian ones, Corsica Ferries and Navarma (Moby Lines) sail mostly from Italian ports like Savona, Genova, La Spezia, and Livorno (the port for Pisa). The fastest is a hydrofoil by Corsica Ferries from Savona. It costs more and takes about three hours. The shortest crossing by standard ferry is from Livorno, and takes four and a half hours. Other routes take longer. But Livorno is at least a half day ride further down the boot of Italy from the Alps and Genova.

Genova and Savona are the ports of embarkation closest to the Alps and central Europe.

Through the Gorges de la Restonica is one of the high mountain roads on the little Mediterranean island of Corsica. Corsica has more roads than a good rider can cover in a week, including passes through mountains like this.

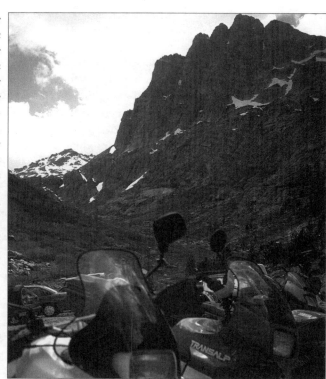

The standard ferries are large ships carrying several decks of trucks and busses and cars towing boats and trailers and lots of motorcycles. They're equipped with restaurants and lounges and maybe movies and pools. Overnight ferries have cabins with a private bath available for much less than most hotel rooms—a good choice. Ferries run on multiple schedules serving multiple ports on Corsica. Not all ports are served every day.

Bastia on the northeast coast of Corsica is the closest to Italy. Calvi on the northwest coast is the closest to France. Ajaccio, the only city on Corsica, is on the southwest coast.

Ferries ply regularly between Bonifacio on the south tip and Sardinia, about an hour boat ride, but a world away.

A daytime ferry practically means overnighting in the port before embarking—not always an attractive option.

Genova and **Savona** are but a half day ride from most any place in the Alps and have the most sailings. Play in the Alps all morning, then cut to the coast. The autostrada leads right to the ports. There is a good **Novotel** right at the otherwise pretty grim port in Genova. You can see the ferry from its windows. And it has safe underground parking; I-16126 Genova; phone: 010 6484; fax: 010 64 8-4844.

Recommended is the overnight ferry from Genova or Savona. Just get there in time for an evening sailing. Crew members secure the bike. Head up to your cabin, clean up. Have a nice dinner. Sleep in a cozy bunk in your private cabin. Get off in the morning for a great riding day on Corsica.

The Corsica ferries always have a lot of motorcycle traffic. Somehow, the word is out among European motorcyclists that Corsica is a great place to ride.

Ferry companies take credit cards and speak English.

Corsica Ferries—Italian offices: Genova, Piazza Dantel 1; phone: 010 59-3301; fax: 010 59-3774. Livorno; phone: 0586 89-8979; fax: 056 89-6103; Savona, Porto Vado, Calata Nord, phone: 019 216-0041; fax: 019 216-0043. In France: Bastia; main reservation office: phone: 0495 32-9595; fax: 0495 32-1471.

Corsica Ferries has agents in Munchen, Zurich, Geneve, and Amsterdam.

Navarma (Moby) Lines: Milano (main office); phone: 0276 01-2502; fax: 0276 01-2175. Genova (agent) Vintiadis Shipping and Travel; phone: 010 20-5651; fax: 010 29-0881. Livorno (agent); L.V. Ghianda; phone: 0586 89-0325; fax: 0586 88-8630.

SNCM Ferryterranee Paris; 12 Rue Godotde Mauroy; F-75009 Paris; phone: 149 24-2424; fax: 149 24-2409. Bastia; phone: 0495 32-8957 or 32-6904; fax: 0495 34-0114 or 32-6909. Nice; phone: 493 13-6699; fax: 0493 13-6681.

Where to Stay

Like western Austria, Corsica is packed with hotels in exotic spots.

Take **Porto,** for instance, on the west coast. It's a tiny village that's a must see and stay, wedged in a crevice between towering pink mountains with surf crashing on pink rocks and good hotels and restaurants and three roads in (and out). Each of the three roads in (and out) rates three stars from Michelin. That's their top rating, and they're right. Mind, it's the roads that get the stars, not some building or other wonder. Each of the three roads is an exhilarating adventure.

At Hotel Les Flots Bleus (the blue waves) each room has a deck facing across water to mountains and the tumble-down watch tower built by the Genovese hundreds of years ago. **Hotel Les Flots Bleus;** F-20150 Porto (Corse); phone: 0495 26-1126; fax: 0495 26-1264.

On the rocks beyond the watch tower is **Hotel Belvedere;** F-20150 Porto; (Corse); phone: 0495 26-1201; fax: 0495 26-1197.

In complete contrast is the Grand Hotel du Monte d'Oro. It's in the forest, all by itself at about 1000 meters elevation just off the main trans-island highway at the Col de Vizza-vona. There's nothing grand about the hotel except its name. It faces the peak it's named after. And they do have snow. There's an old part to the hotel and a newer part. Neither would rate high on the amenities scale. But the lounge has a huge fireplace and lots of overstuffed chairs. Meals are family style. It's fun. **Grand Hotel du Monte d'Oro;** F-20219 Vizzavona; phone: 0495 47-2106 or 47-2344; fax: 0495 21-8228.

Twenty-five kilometers west and across a pass from Bastia is **St. Florent,** one of the few Corsican villages with a French name. It has a yacht basin, waterfront restaurants, and several hotels. One is the **Hotel Dolce Notte** (sweet night) directly on the beach (a bit rocky) on the edge of the village. F-20217 St. Florent (Corse); phone: 0495 37-0665; fax: 0495 37-1070. The hotel has no restaurant, but serves breakfast on your patio, directly on the water.

Porto Vecchio is on the southeast coast, with a medieval town on the hill and newer stuff around its yacht basin. There's the **Hotel Shegara;** F-20137 Porto Vecchio (Corse); phone: 0495 70-0431; fax: 0495 70-2338.

Hotel Solemare is down at the southern point of Corsica at Bonifacio. The hotel faces the massive ancient walled city across the fjord-like harbor. F-20169 Bonifacio (Corse); phone: 0495 73-0106; fax: 0495 73-1257.

A few kilometers north of Porto Vecchio is a small village named **Favona.** Right on its curving white sand beach is **Hotel U Dragulinu.** The Mediterranean is crystal clear and the lounges on the sand have umbrellas and soft pads. Dinner and breakfast diners can look out on the waves. Maybe the first course for dinner will be wonderful mussels. U Dra-gulinu; F-20144 Favona; phone: 0495 73-2030; fax: 0495 73-2206.

Most hotel operators will insist that bikes be parked in a locked garage at night. A good idea.

The first Corsica trip, below, starts as if you had just arrived on Corsica. The trips following, Trips 2 through 8, are from the base communities listed above.

Trip 61   Col de Vergio to Porto

Distance	*190 kilometers*
Terrain	*Mountain roads, some very narrow*
Highlights	*Delightful villages, some asleep; a couple of medieval relics; pine and chestnut forests, exotic gorges; ★Col de Vergio (1477 meters)*

Leave Bastia or Calvi following the signs for St. Florent. It's only 25 kilometers and a pass (Col de Teghime) away from Bastia. Just a little farther from Calvi. From Bastia, the road climbs aggressively and tight even while still in town. Toward St. Florent it passes through vineyards. If you're coming from an overnight ferry, St. Florent is a great place for breakfast. Right on the little main square is a *patisserie* serving fresh croissants and breakfast.

Take the tiny road going south from the little square (not the main one west of town). It is very rural. In about 5 kilometers it passes a 12th century church, still a cathedral, called Nebbio. There's nobody there, but it's worth a look. Here is a perfectly preserved Romanesque style building built by the best artisans Pisa could send.

Past **Nebbio,** climb on up the mountain road through open countryside to Oletta and on to **Murato.** Murato sits upon the crest of the island with views to the Mediterranean on the east and west. And there is a little black and white stone church (they couldn't decide whether to make it black and white stripes, or black and white checkerboard) built about the same time as the cathedral below, and a delightful contrast in craftsmanship. (It helps to remember that Pisa was building its cathedral and leaning tower about the same time in black and white, and seems to have been more ambitious, although Murato's tower doesn't lean quite enough to be famous.)

The road south from Murato to **Ponte Leccia** has just been paved—one narrow lane with a center stripe. Wide pavement buffs may want to backtrack a couple of kilometers and take the wild ride down the Defile de Lancone to the east coast, and then follow the signs south and west in the direction of Corte and Ajaccio.

Before either, but after climbing into the mountains, just nine kilometers south of Ponte Leccia (there is a bridge) leave the main highway and head west to Porto. First comes the awesome **Scala de Santa Regina,** a gorge with the road barely hung on the edge. Then pine forests and the **Col de Vergio** with a monument figure. Heading down west the forest turns to chestnut, the forest d'Aitone. Pigs like chestnuts. There may be some.

Below the forest, the road enters the **Gorges de Spelunca,** majestic walls and formations in pink. Somehow, the road has to get to the bottom of the gorge.

On the way down is a little village, **Evisa,** with a hotel restaurant called **Scopa Rossa.** F-20126 Evisa. There are several pull-out view sites.

At the bottom and mouth of the gorge is Porto. Everything is still pink, except the eucalyptus trees.

Some American bikers came upon some German bikers climbing the Col de Vergio. All but one of the Germans took the bait and played across the pass, stopping at a pull-out view spot. Finally, the holdout rode up and immediately fell over. Rushing to assist, the Americans noted the rider's leg alarmingly crumpled under the bike. "Not to worry," said the German, in English, "it isn't mine." It was a prosthesis.

Trip 62 Calvi

• •

Distance   *160 kilometers (it'll take all day)*

Terrain   *Very, very tight, twisting roads. No highway speed possible*

Highlights *Wild mountains and coast to Calvi, a medieval walled city with busy waterfront cafes and promenades*

Take the coast road north from Porto, climbing the cliffs with views down over the village and gulf. Cross the **Col de la Croix.** Returning from Calvi, a bit better time can be maintained by taking the inland road south.

Trip 63   Les Calanche

Distance	*100 kilometers*
Terrain	*Some tight, narrow road, but mostly more open two lane*
Highlights	*More exotic pink rock formations and rocky coastline; beautiful beaches and forested mountain pass; Col de Sevi (1094 meters)*

Follow the **Les Calanche** road south from Porto. The formations and the road will require some stopping and picture taking. Unbelievable. On through Cargese and down to the coast at **Sagone** which has a wonderful broad white sand beach. At the south end of the beach is a tiny hotel restaurant with a sublime location. **La Marine;** F-20118 Sagone; phone: 0495 28-0003; fax: 0495 28-0398.

Head northwest on the inland road from Sagone, climbing over the **Col de Sevi,** and connecting with the Gorges de Spelunca road back down to Porto.

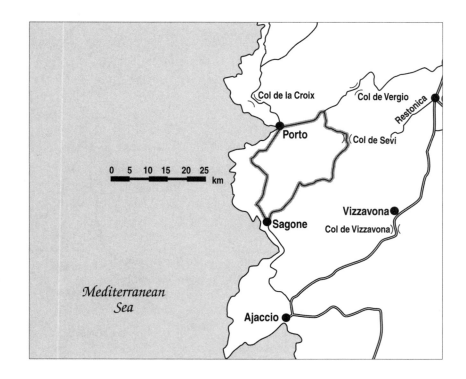

Trip 64 Bonifacio

· ·

Distance	*190 kilometers*
Terrain	*Fairly open, smooth, two lane coastal roads, then some tight mountain stuff*
Highlights	*The walled city of Bonifacio, fjord-like harbor, clifftop view of Sardinia, yacht-filled waterfront at Propriano, prehistoric carvings at Filitosa, mountain roads and villages*

Drive right up the steep road and in through the arched gate in the massive walls of Bonifacio. Through the village and on the clifftop, it's possible to see Sardinia and the crashing waves far below. Note the tiny stairway up the massive cliff that was supposed to give besieged villagers access to the sea.

The very narrow harbor between cliffs, north of the walled city, is where the Sardinia ferries dock.

It's a rather uneventful trip north roughly along the west coast to **Propriano** with its active yacht harbor, on the far side of which is the shoreline road toward **Filitosa,** site of prehistoric carvings.

From Propriano climb the mountain roads east to **Zonza,** then on around the lake and forests of l'Ospedale, over the **Col de Taglio Maggiore** with views of the east coast, then sweep on down to Porto Vecchio.

Trip 65 Vizzavona and Restonica

Distance	*80 kilometers*
Terrain	*Some very tight, twisty roads*
Highlights	*Climb through forests alongside rushing mountain streams to a high mountain bowl at 1300 meters;* ★*Col de Vizzavona (1163 meters)*

Cross the **Col de Vizzavona** and ride north on the main road as far as Corte, the historic capital of independent Corsica. **Restonica** is signed west from Corte. There's a hotel and several rustic restaurants along the narrow, one lane wide road which ends in a peak-rimmed mountain bowl.

From Corte back to Vizzavona, try going a few kilometers down the main road southeast (through a grove of cork trees) and then climb back over the **Col de Bellagranajo.**

Trip 66   Col de Verde and Col de Bavella

•••

Distance	*225 kilometers (a long day)*
Terrain	*Mostly rough paved, narrow, tight mountain roads*
Highlights	*Wandering mountain roads with remote villages and a couple of good passes, especially the Col de Verde (1289 meters) and the ★Col de Bavella (1218 meters), Col de Sorba (1311 meters)*

From Vizzavona ride north a few kilometers and then turn east over the **Col de Sorba,** wandering through forest to the mountain village of **Ghisoni.** Ghisoni has a few commercial establishments, and each will be pleased to see customers. The road works (that's the right term) its way on south through woods and past small waterfalls over the Col de Verde, finally reaching **Aullene,** a mountain crossroad village with restaurants and services. Go east from Aullene crossing a canyon and climbing back up to Zonza where all of a sudden, and inexplicably, there's a fine sweeping highway northerly up the **Col de Bavella.** The top of the col, in a pine forest, has several attractive restaurants and views across miles of island and sea. Just to make a point, the road down the northeast side of the col to the coast is rough and rutted (paved more or less). It traverses wild forests with views of Dolomite-like peaks. Once down on the east coast, follow the main road (pretty fast for a change) north to **Ghisonaccia** (17 kilometers), and then head inland (west) climbing through the Defile de l'Inzecca and Stretta and over the Col de Sorba back to Vizzavona.

Trip 67   St. Florent

•••

Distance   *180 kilometers*

Terrain   *Mountains and desert and forest*

Highlights *Ski bowl at 1450 meters, desert that looks like southern California (but just a few kilometers of it) with more twisty mountain roads*

The main road southwest from St. Florent crosses the Desert des Agriates that seems like the desert mountains of southern California, except that there's that sea out there. The road is sort of tortured for about twenty-five kilometers. Then it joins the main road heading inland (southeasterly). Make time, maybe speed, toward Ponte Leccia, just before which there's a small road that follows the **Gorges de l'Asco** southwesterly into a high mountain bowl. It's about thirty kilometers one way to the bowl where there is a bar restaurant.

Back at Ponte Leccia, cross the main Bastia-Ajaccio highway and head southeasterly up the small mountain road to **Morosaglia,** climbing over some minor cols and finally wending down to the main road on the east coast. Then it's probably best to head north to Bastia and across to St. Florent.

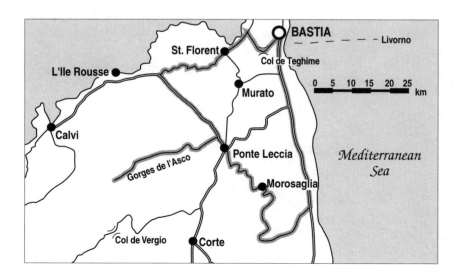

Trip 68 Cap Corse

Distance	*170 kilometers*
Terrain	*Tight, twisting roads along rugged coast*
Highlights	*Similar to California Highway One north of San Francisco, except more precipitous*

Cap Corse is the name usually given to the whole mountainous finger that projects about fifty kilometers north from Bastia and St. Florent. There's nothing flat on the finger. One road circles it following the coastal cliffs as best it can. Sometimes there are little clusters of houses along the road. Sometimes they are far below on the beach with minimal trails down to them. Start out on the road north from St. Florent. The only recommended detour down to the water is at the north end. A windy loop road goes right down to the water at the northernmost point of Corsica with a cluster of buildings known as **Barcaggio.**

Then the main loop road around Cap Corse actually gets down to the beach on the east coast at Macinaggio which happens to have a nice row of waterfront restaurants.

There are two transpeninsular roads that climb across the mountains from coast to coast. They're roughly parallel. So it's possible to take one, and come back on the other. The more northerly one is just four kilometers south of Macinaggio at **Marine de Meria.** The second climbs back over the **Col de Santa Lucie** and gets back to the east coast at **Marine de Luri.**

Then follow south along the east coast, which is a pleasantly sweeping highway, to Bastia, and home to St. Florent.

The roads around Cap Corse, the north finger of Corsica, have much in common with Higway One in California. But Cap Corse and its roads are much more rugged.

On the roads around Andermatt, it's possible to ride one exotic pass after another, without ever getting mixed up with cities or dense traffic. Here, the north side of the Grimsel Pass snakes down to Gletsch, no more than a couple of stone buildings, where the Furka Pass road starts climbing back up and east to Andermatt. (See Trips 1-4.)

Special Little Roads

In the Alps are many special little roads that might have been put there just for motorcyclists to play on. It has taken me many enjoyable years to discover them; this book is my tribute to the joy they have given me. For your convenience, they are arranged according to the regions they occupy. But some of these roads are so exceptional, their potential for enjoyment so great, that they deserve to be singled out and given special consideration by any motorcyclist.

All the roads I'll mention here are described elsewhere in the book, in their appropriate geographical context. Most of them don't go anywhere in particular, certainly nowhere of commercial importance. They are not necessarily high or awesome, although some are both. Most of them have stretches that are only one lane wide. They are all paved. Some of them are short and some long. Some remain obscure even though they're close to major tourist areas or routes.

Special Little Roads in Switzerland

1. Pragel Pass between the towns of Glarus and Schwyz. (Part of Andermatt Trip 4.)

2. Glaubenbuelen Pass between the towns of Schupfheim and Giswil. (Part of The Berner Oberland Trip 6.)

3. Glaubenberg Pass between the towns of Entlebuch and Sarnen. (Also part of The Berner Oberland Trip 6.)

Special Little Roads in France

1. Cormet de Roselend and Col du Pre between the towns of Bourg St. Maurice and Beaufort. (Part of Trip 13, Mont Blanc region.)

2. Col de Joux Plane between the towns of Morzine and Samoens. (Part of Trip 15, Lac d'Annecy region.)

3. Col Agnel between Guillestre in France and Sampeyre in Italy. (Part of Trip 19, The Southern Alps.)

Special Little Roads in Italy

1. Colle San Carlo between the towns of Morgex and La Thuile. (Part of Trip 13, Mont Blanc region.)

2. Passo di Croce Domini between the towns of Bagolino and Breno. (Part of Trip 37, Riva and Lago di Garda.)

3. Passo di Vivione between the towns of Forno Allione and Shilpario. (Part of Trip 37, Riva and Lago di Garda.)

4. Wurz Joch (Passo di Erbe) between the towns of St. Martin and Bressanone (Brixen). (Part of Trip 34, Sud Tirol, and Trip 42, The Dolomites.)

5. Passo Manghen between the towns of Cavalese and Borgo. (Part of Trip 42, The Dolomites.)

6. Col di Sampeyre between Sampeyre and Donero. (Part of Trip 19, The Southern Alps.)

7. Passo Duran between Villa and Agordo. (Part of Trip 41, Southern Dolomites.)

Special Little Roads in Austria

1. Furka Joch between the towns of Rankweil and Damuls. (Part of Trip 41, Liechtenstein, Santis, and the Arlberg.)

2. Hahntenn Joch between the towns of Imst and Elmen. (Part of Trip 48, Austrian Tirol.)

3. Haiming Joch between the village of Haiming and Ochsengarten. (Part of Trip 48, Austrian Tirol.)

4. Zillertaler Hohenstrasse between the towns of Ried and Ramsberg. (Part of Trip 52, Austria East of the Tirol.)

If You Have Only a Little Time

It's better to ride a little in the Alps than not at all. So if you just have a few days, which country, which roads, should you aim for? Where will you have the most fun and see the most in just a few days? A week?

First Andermatt, Switzerland. It's covered right at the beginning of this book. The mountains are spectacular, the roads exciting, facilities plentiful, and there's no big city traffic to worry about. You can get to the area quickly by Autobahn, and then leave the Autobahn and traffic behind. There are several full days of riding around Andermatt.

Second, the Dolomites in northern Italy. They're covered in the section of the same name. Like those around Andermatt, the mountains are special and the roads are right up in them. Facilities are plentiful, and there is no big city traffic. You can get there quickly from the Brennero Autostrada. Several more full days of riding.

Just remember the warning in the front of this book. Alpinitis is contagious.

Other European Goals

Are all the great roads in the Alps? Aren't there any others?

Of course. But truly, all suffer in comparison to the Alps. Try the roads anywhere else, as many have. They may seem pretty good. Sometimes the scenery is almost as good. Then come back to the Alps. There's no getting around it. The roads of the Alps are the best. Nothing compares. Except Corsica.

Other areas tested, in no particular order:

Norway

A real challenge. There is a lot of it, about 2400 kilometers from Oslo to the North Cape. And there's almost nobody there. Cruise posters illustrate how lovely the fjords are. They don't show how tedious and occasional the roads are. There is lots of water. But facilities are few, modest, and very expensive. One-lane roads with trucks and buses going both ways cling to the edges of the fjords. An overlay of skid marks is a constant reminder of what may be around endless blind corners. From the fjords, the roads climb up into a tundra-like crossing to the next fjord. And Norway is a long haul from the core of Europe.

It's possible to cut some of the travel time to and from Norway by using ferries from Newcastle in the north of England or from the Netherlands, to Bergen; or from Kiel, in north Germany to Oslo. All of the ferry connections take about 18 hours. However, It's also possible to fast ferry in 2-1/2 hours from Hirtshals, Denmark, to Kristiansand, on Norway's south coast, where Beach's Motorcycle Adventures (see their listing on page 270) offers motorcycle tours or independent bike rentals throughout Norway. For about the price of a night in a modest hotel (less than any hotel in Norway), it's possible to get a tiny cabin on the ferry and eliminate a bunch of flat road time to boot. It is heady to ride all night in daylight. There can be a bit of a high about 1 a.m.

Pyrenees

Every once in a while, the high mountains that separate Spain and France look almost Alpine. A few of the passes are Alpine in height, and some of the snow bowls could double for those in the Alps. What's missing is the culture and the road network. The tiny independent country of Andorra has adequate facilities, and some, up above its main valley road, are very pleasant. As a tax-free country, it is jammed with tourists loading their cars with everything imaginable (including new motorcycles), and with trucks hauling the stuff in so the tourists can buy it and haul it out. Americans are unknown in Andorra. The Spanish side is no longer cheap.

Sardinia (Sardegna)

Visible from the south of Corsica, Sardinia is not nearly as rugged, and doesn't make the cut.

★ Isle of Man

Since the first years of the 20th century, the first week of June has been motorcycle week on the Isle of Man. The adjective for it is Manx, for cats and for Nortons. The island is in the Irish Sea, west of England, north of Wales, and east of Ireland. The collection of enthusiasts from all over the world is a joy to be part of. The major TT races are the first weekend of June, with practice during the prior week. Practice can be as much fun as the racing. The course is all public roads about the island, totaling about 30 miles. It's open to the public except during practice hours and during races. The course is open to all on the first Sunday in June. It's come to be known as Mad Sunday, as too many amateurs overestimate their skills. The atmosphere is motorcycle-friendly.

Accommodations are working-class British, as is the food. The island has some nice roads to explore besides the course. Access is by ferry from Heysham on the Lancashire coast of England, north of Liverpool, with a weekly run from Dublin. Both take about five hours. Reservations for the ferry are essential, and can be obtained from the Isle of Man Steam Packet Company in Douglas, phone: 01624 661661; fax: 01624 645697; e-mail: res@steam-packet.com. Accommodation information is available from the Isle of Man Tourist

Board, phone: 01624 686766; or at their website: www.isle-of-man.com. They do indeed speak English there, but they drive on the left, even on the TT course.

Nurburgring

The historic and famous Nurburgring is often available to riders. It's much longer than most tracks, the north ring being about 14 kilometers, and it sweeps and wiggles through the low Eifel Mountains up near the border of Belgium, about 40 kilometers west of Koblenz. (It's easy for the English speaker to confuse the Nurburgring up north with the Bayrisch city, Nurnberg, where the war crimes trials were held after World War II.)

Many Americans have participated in the driving school held over a period of several days each summer on the Nurburgring by the BMW Clubs of Europe. Contact Werner Briel in Mulheim am der Ruhr; phone: 020 335-8020; fax: 020 337-6372; e-mail: SchultenHL@t-online.de. The school concentrates on learning the multitudinous curves of the Ring. A reasonable beginning competence is presumed. It's a good place to make European contacts.

▲▲ So, How About a Bike?

There are several ways to have a bike in the Alps. Each depends on two factors that the user decides: time and money. Usually, a little of one will save a bit of the other.

- borrow or rent
- buy
- ship it from home
- keep a bike there

Borrow or Rent One

It surely would be nice to have a friend in Europe to borrow a bike from. Lacking that, you can rent one.

Bikes are available for rent from many sources. Most of the tour operators who are known in the United States rent bikes to riders who attend their tours. However, several tour operators will also rent motorcycles to riders who are not on tour with them.

BMW rents (and sells and services) from its Niederlassungs (that's an Anglicised plural of Niederlassungen), its company-owned subsidiaries located in several major cities, including Munchen. The BMW "factory," the museum and office tower are near the Olympic Center on Peutel Ring in Munchen. BMW Niederlassung Munchen is north of that on Frankfurter Ring. (Both are easily accessible by U-Bahn, subway.) Phone: 089 35-6210; fax: 089 356-21499. The Niederlassungs have several rental plans and several kinds of bikes available. They accept credit cards.

Several rental sources advertise in America.

Bosenberg Motorcycle Excursions in Bad Kreuznach, Germany; phone: 067 16-7580; fax: 067 16-7153; e-mail: bosenberg@compuserve.com.

Knopf Motorcycle Touring in Heidelberg, Germany; phone and fax: 062 217-8213; e-mail:knopftours@aol.com Knopf will meet arrivals at the Frankfurt airport.

Motor Center Thun, Switzerland; phone: 033 439-5959; fax: 033 439-5950; website: www.moto-center.ch.

Court Fisher of BMW Motorcycle Owners of America makes a continuous and experienced study of the motorcycle scene in Europe. Details about shipping, renting and insuring and buying are constantly changing and he reports the shifts almost monthly in the *BMW Owners News.* He is most congenial about sharing his hard-learned information from his home in Princeton, N.J., phone 609 924-1773.

Members of Harley Owners Group can make arrangements to rent a Harley in Europe through H.O.G. in Milwaukee.

Bikes can also be rented from a Honda dealer in Switzerland: Grisoni; CH-7302 Landquart; phone: 81 322-7288; fax: 81 322-6615. Landquart is in Graubunden, east of Zurich.

A rental from any of these sources should be ready to ride; serviced, good tires, insured.

Buy One There

Some factors beyond the control of individuals, and even dealers and manufacturers, bear on the choice, and they vary from year to year and season to season.

The rate of exchange is crucial, along with the rules and cost of shipping. In some years American currencies are high and that makes everything in Europe, including motorcycles, seem like a bargain. In such circumstances, shipping a bike from America won't make much sense since they're cheaper in Europe than America and almost all bikes are available for sale.

Then the opposite happens. American currency sinks in relative value and everything is cheaper in America. It then may make sense to ship your bike from America.

There has been one mitigating factor in this game: until now, BMW had not changed its price for factory-delivered machines as fast as the currency had changed. So when dollars were weak, BMW held the price in dollars, with the result that the price for a European-delivered U.S.-specification bike was actually much less than the Europeans were paying for the same machine at the same place and time. And vice versa. When American currency went up in value, it was cheaper to buy on the open market in Europe. There is talk that BMW may terminate its European delivery program in 1998.

If the program continues, arrangements must be made through a US dealer. The most experienced is in New York: Joel Sacher; phone: 516 427-4045.

Then there's the matter of U.S. specifications. Only the manufacturer can certify to them, and it's practically impossible to get a non-U.S.-spec bike into the U.S. Of course, if the goal is to leave the bike in Europe, then U.S. specs are not so important, unless U.S. registration is desired.

To buy a BMW, the best arrangement has been with a local BMW dealer at home. The price for factory delivery should be the same from any source, unless the dollar should soar in relative value. It might be worthwhile to call Paddy Maddock near Dublin, Ireland. Phone: 1 286-8418; fax: 1 286-3841 (country code 353). That language he speaks is English.

Dealers all over Europe are selling new and used bikes. Magazines and papers are full of ads, just like in America. Investing some time and patience can result in a good deal. Europeans do have strict vehicle inspection, called TUV in German, that limits modifications and maintains safety and pollution controls. They also have a significant value-added tax. A dealer selling to a non-resident alien should be able to take care of everything including insurance, and possibly, the refund of the value-added tax upon proof of export.

Ship a Bike From Home

Shipping from America can be a good deal, but it's an ever-changing game. What worked well one time may not the next. Shipping by sea, short of taking a bike as baggage, takes time and planning. Usually the bike must be crated, and then it must be forklift handled to the dock, and the process reversed at the other end. Docks are often inconveniently located. Rats can eat the plastic! Freighters may not be on an exact schedule, so time at both ends is required.

So air freight is almost always the choice. With most airlines, bikes must be crated to be flown, but not with Lufthansa. They have had lots of experience shipping motorcycles and know how to transport them safely without crating. They require that you travel on the same flight as your bike. It is fun to get off the airplane in Europe, go around to the freight terminal, go through customs, and ride away from the airport. Agents for other carriers are hungry for business, and are willing to talk both price and crating. Sometimes containers can hold several bikes for the price of one. Prices are related to cubic space needed.

The airline and agent that worked wonders one time may not the next. Call a variety of airline freight agents. One of them may be a biker. If you're planning on bringing the bike back to the U.S., arrange both ways at the same time.

Michael Mandell in New York and Warren Motorcycle Transport in Florida specialize in arranging the shipping of motorcycles by air.

Mandell; phone: 800 245-8726; fax: 516 822-0172.

Warren; phone: 800 443-7519; fax: 954 726-7336.

To get your bike out of customs in Europe, it will be necessary to prove you have European insurance (see "Good Stuff to Know"), and the customs agent will want to be assured that the bike is just passing through, not being imported. If the bike is legal in America, then it's legal for an American to operate it on holiday in Europe.

If the bike is ever sold to a European, then it will have to be imported with all the taxes and inspections Europeans require.

Keep a Bike in Europe

Sometimes it's harder to find a good air freight deal back from Europe to America. Many Americans are so hooked that they keep bikes in Europe from one holiday to the next. Some rent garages. Some leave them in bonded warehouses. Some leave bikes with cooperative dealers. Then the only problem is how to keep the thing registered in America, while avoiding permanently importing it to Europe.

An Organized Tour?

Most every road is better shared. It's possible to meet new lifelong motorcycle friends on an organized tour. Other smart, creative, attractive, motorcycle crazies like you. If time is limited, the tour folk will take care of the details and leave the riding to you. They just may have some good ideas

Motorcycling with a group will introduce you to other like-minded adventurers. Many friendships made through motorcycling last a lifetime. And what better way to savor the adventure than to share it with friends. Here, a group checks its route through Passo di Tremalzo, above Pieve. (See Trip 36.)

about where to go and how to get there. And they've had practice helping if something should not go as planned.

Tours are a good bet for anyone with limited time and/or Euro-riding experience. You meet the nicest people . . . .

Recently, an American couple riding a very narrow and rarely traveled Italian pass (Vivione, Trip 37) sideswiped a protruding rock. It split the transmission housing. For anyone traveling independently, that might have been the end of the trip. Their next worry would have been how to get themselves and the busted bike down out of the boondocks. Then, how to get the bike fixed. Then what to do while it's getting fixed. In this case, the couple was on a Beach trip. The Beach luggage van carries a cellphone. A phone call was made, the bike stashed beside the road, and the couple continued to the next hotel aboard other tour members' bikes. Later, after delivering all the luggage, the Beach van took off for the little pass and retrieved the bike. Next day, the couple continued their trip on a different bike.

Here are several tour operators who specialize in trips through the Alps. They'll even carry the hair dryer.

Beach's Motorcycle Adventures, Ltd.
2763 West River Parkway
Grand Island, NY 14072-2053
Phone: (716) 773-4960
Fax: (716) 773-5227
E-mail: bmastaff@buffnet.net
Web site: bma.buffnet.net

Bosenberg Motorcycle Excursions
Mainzer Strasse 54
D-6550 Bad Kreuznach
GERMANY
Phone: (49) 671-67312
Fax: (49) 671-67153
E-mail: bosenberg@compuserve.com
Web site: www.bosenberg.com

Edelweiss Bike Travel
Steinreichweg 1
A-6414 Mieming
AUSTRIA
Phone: (43) 526-45690
US Phone: (800) 877-2784
Fax: (43) 526-458533
E-mail: edelweiss@tirol.com
Web site: www.netwing.at//bike_travel

European Adventures
2 The Circle, Bryn Newydd
Prestatyn, Clwyd LL19 9EU
WALES
Phone: (44) 745 85-3455
Fax: (44) 745 88-8919

Jed Halpern's S.A.P. Tour
(Swiss Alps and Passes Tour)
Route du Simplon 35A; CH-1907 Saxon
SWITZERLAND
Phone: (41) 79 225-1988
Fax: (41) 27 744-3073
E-mail: saptour@bluewin.ch
Web site: ourworld.compuserve.com/homepages/goldwing_tours/

mhs Motorradtouren GmbH
Donnersbergerstrasse 32
D-80634 Munich
GERMANY
Phone: (49) 89 168-4888
Fax: (49) 89 166-5549
E-mail: motorradtouren.mhs@t-online.de
Web site: www.motorrad.reisen.de

Muenchner Freiheit
Postfach 44 01 48
D-8000 Munich 44
GERMANY
Phone: (49) 89 39-5768
Fax: (49) 89 34-4832
E-mail: MuenchnerFreiheit@compuserve.com
Web site: www.motorrad.bmw.de/erlebniswelt/fernreisen

Team Aventura
Karlsebene 2
D-8924 Steingaden
GERMANY
Phone: (49) 8 862-6161
Fax: (49) 8 862-6161

Von Thielmann Tours
P.O. Box 87764
San Diego, CA 92138
Phone: 619 463-7788 or 619 234-1558
Fax: 619 463-7788
E-mail: 105114.3154@compuserve.com

World Motorcycle Tours
7106 NW 108th Avenue
Tamarac, FL 33321
Phone: (800) 443-7519 or (954) 726-0494
Fax: (954) 726-7336
E-mail: bikeship@icanect.net

Glossary

aiguille - French word for needle, applied especially to peaks in the Mt. Blanc massif, as Aiguille du Midi

albergo - Italian word for inn or small hotel

Allemagne - the French word for Germany

Alpenglow - the almost flourescent pink glow of snow covered peaks at sunrise and sunset.

Alpenstrasse - German, a road in the Alps, plural is Alpenstrassen

Alpinist - a mountain climber in the Alps; alpinist is a mountain climber in general

Alpinitis - a Hermannism, infected by the Alps

alt, alte - German word for old

aperto - Italian word for open

Apfel - German word for apple

aubergine - French word for eggplant

Ausfahrt - German word for freeway exit (a pedestrian exit is Ausgang)

Ausstellung - German word for exhibition

Autobahn - German word for freeway; plural is Autobahnen

autoroute - French word for freeway

autostrada - Italian word for freeway, plural is autostrade

aux - French preposition, "to the;" hotel Aux Mille Etoiles, Les Marecottes (CH)

bain - French word for bath

basilica - a special name for a large church; not a cathedral

Bayern - German word for Bavaria

Bayrisch - adj. German word for Bavarian

bei - German word, prep. for at or near; Trimbach bei Olten

Berghaus - German for house on a mountain; Berghaus Gurnigel (CH)

Bergstrasse - German for mountain road; Bergstrasse Ferrenau (A)

Berner - German word for Bernese, adj. of Bern (CH)

Bernese - adj. & n. pertaining to Bern

besonder - German word for special

bis - German word, prep., until

bleu - French word for blue

bolognese - Italian adjective for the town Bologna, often applied to a meat sauce on pasta

bourg - French word for village

Brot - German word for bread

Brucke - German word for bridge

Bundesstrasse - German for federal road, *i.e.,* not a freeway

cambio - Italian word for change, exchange

campanile - bell tower

cannelloni - a kind of pasta

cappuccino - Italian coffee with steamed milk

carne - Italian word for meat, flesh

centro - Italian word for center, downtown

certosa - Italian word for charterhouse; Hotel Certosa (I) near Merano, called Karthaus in German

chiuso - Italian word for closed, shut, locked

cognoscente - a connoisseur, one in the know

col - French word for pass, as a mountain pass

corso - Italian word for course, large street; *in corso* is Italian for in progress

creme de la creme - the very choicest

Cyrillic - Slavic alphabet, Russian

Danemark - German word for Denmark; Coupe Danemark, hot fudge sundae

del - Italian "of the" masculine before a consonant

della - Italian "of the" feminine before consonant, singular

demi - French word for half

der - German word for article "the," masculine

des - French prep., "of the"

Deutsch - German word for German; adj., requires declension; Deutsche Alpenstrasse

Deutschland - (D) German word for Germany

deviazione - Italian word for detour

di - Italian word, prep. "of," "by," "with"

d' - French prep., "of," before a vowel

Dolomiten - German word for Dolomites

Dolomiti - Italian word for Dolomites

Dorf - German word for village

drei - German word for three

Edelweiss - German name for Alpine flower

einfach - German word for simple

Eisenbahn - German word for railroad; name of a
     restaurant known as motorcycle meeting place (CH)

Eisenwaren - German word for hardware

Eis - German word for ice, also ice cream

entrecot - French for sirloin steak

etoile - French word for star, pl. etoiles

Euro - prefix for European

Fahrrad - German word for bicycle

ferme - French word for closed

formaggio - Italian word for cheese; often Parmesan

forno - Italian word for furnace, oven; al forno means
     baked

franc - French and Swiss unit of money

frei - German word for free, vacant; Zimmer Frei, room for
     rent

Furstentum - German word for principality; Furstentum
     Liechtenstein (FL)

Furst - German word for prince

Gasthaus - German word for inn

Gasthof - German word for inn

gelateria - Italian word for ice cream parlor

gelato - Italian word for ice cream

gemutlich - German word for comfortable

Gemutlichkeit - German word for coziness

Germania - Italian name for Germany

glace - French word for ice, ice cream

grosse - German adj., big

Hauser - German word for houses, plural of Haus

haut, haute - French adjective for high

Heidi - German woman's name; fictional Alpine story for
     children

heiss - German word for hot

Hochalpenstrasse - German for high Alpine road

Hochberghaus - German for high mountain house

hoch - German word for high

Hof - German word for court, court yard, yard, as in
     Gasthof

Hohe - German word for height

Hohenstrasse - German for high road

Hutte - German word for hut, a mountain refuge

insalata - Italian word for salad

Italia - (I) Italian word for Italy

Joch - German word for yoke, often applied to a pass

joli - French word for pretty

Kaiser Schmarrn - sweet Austrian dessert

Kalte - German word for cold (coldness)

Kaserne - German word for barracks

Kirche - German word for church

Konige - German word for kings

Konigschloss - German word for royal castle, palace

Kurort - German word for health resort, also see Aflenz
    Kurort

lac - French word for lake

lago - Italian word for lake

lavoro - Italian word for work, labor

le, les - French word for "the," singular and plural

linguini - pasta

lira - Italian unit of money

magno - Italian word for great; see Campo Carlo Magno

malhereusement - French word for unhappily

Mark - German unit of money

marmottes - mountain animal; Les Marmottes, a restaurant
    in La Thuile (I)

massif - a principle mountain

militaire - French word for military; see Route Militaire

mille - French word for thousand, see Les Mille Etoiles

Mitte - German word for middle, center, Stadtmitte means
    downtown

Montessori - Italian educator

Motorrad - German word for motorcycle; German
    motorcycle bi-monthly; plural is Motorrader

Moto Sport Schweiz - Swiss motorcycle weekly

Munchs - German motorcycle brand

Nasse - German word for wet

nazionale - Italian word for national

neu - German word for new

Novembre - Italian for November

ober - German word for upper

Osterreich - German name for Austria

ost - German word for east

ouvert - French word for open

parco - Italian word for park

parmesan - Italian variety of cheese

passo - Italian word for pass
Perrier - bottled water from France
Pinzgau - region (A) S of Salzburg
pomodoro - Italian word for tomato
ponte - Italian word for bridge
pre - prefix denoting priority
Prix - French word for prize
Puch - Austrian motorcycle
Rader - plural of Rad, German word for wheel
rifugio - Italian mountain refuge
ristorante - Italian word for restaurant
Rivella - a bottled soft drink in Switzerland
Romansch - the language of Graubunden (CH)
sacrario - Italian word for sanctuary, cemetery
Sattel - German word for saddle or pass
Schlucht - German word for gorge
Schweinshax'n - typical Austrian and Bavarian cut of pork
Schweiz - German word for Switzerland
See - German word for lake
Semmelknodel - an Austrian and Bavarian dumpling
Sinalco - soft drink in Switzerland
Sonne - German word for sun
Spezi - soft drink in Austria and Bavaria
Spitze - German word for top, tip, point; Edelweiss Spitze
Stadt - German word for city
Stau See - German word for reservoir created by a dam
Strasse - German word for road or street
sud - German word for south
Suisse - French name for Switzerland
Svizzera - Italian name for Switzerland
tagliatelli - pasta
Tal - German word for valley
telepherique - French word for cable car
terme - Italian word for hot spring
Tiroler - German for pertaining to Tirol
Toffel Strudel - an Austrian dessert
Toffler - Swiss German for motorcyclist
Toff - Swiss German word for motorcycle
Tofftreffpunkt - Swiss German for a motorcycle meeting
   place
Tor - German word for gate
tortellini - pasta

toutes - French word for all; toutes directions means all directions

trattoria - an Italian word for restaurant

tre - Italian word for three

Tyrol - English spelling of Tirol

Uberwachung - German word for oversee, supervise; Besonder Uberwachung means special supervision

Umleitung - German word for detour

und - German word for and

val - Italian, short for valle (valley)

valle - Italian for valley

Verkehrsburo - German for travel bureau

Versicherung - German word for insurance

viale - Italian word for avenue

vietato - Italian word for forbidden

vorder - German word for front

vous - French word for you

vue - French word for view

Wald - German word for forest

WC - common sign for toilet (Water Closet)

wechseln - German word for change, exchange

weiss - German word for white

Wienerschnitzel - cutlet (meat) Viennese style

Wurst - German word for sausage

Zimmer - German word for room; Zimmer Frei means room for rent

Index

●●

Riding in the Alps takes energy, like a Coupe Danemark (a hot fudge sundae). John replenishes his reserves on the terrace of Hotel Rhodannenberg overlooking Klon Taler See, on Pragel Pass in Switzerland. (See Trip 4.)

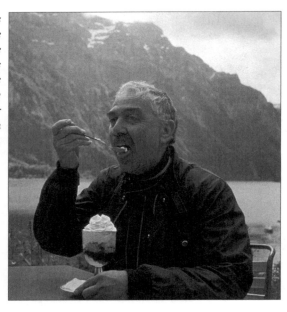

About the Author

John Hermann started riding motorcycles in 1960. His love affair with the Alps began the same year, when he took two car trips through the region that convinced him that the best way to experience Alpine roads would be by motorcycle. In 1970, he took off on a solo trip via a European-delivered BMW, only to discover that a bike trip through the Alps required more planning, understanding, and skills than he'd anticipated.

In 1975, Hermann returned to the Alps as part of a motorcycle tour organized by Beach's Motorcycle Adventures. Even though he rode early and late every day of the Beach trip, he couldn't try all the roads begging to be explored. So he left his bike in Europe and returned later that year for more.

That's been his pattern ever since: one or two trips to the Alps every year. Over the past 23 years he's explored every nook and cranny of the Alps as well as every other part of Europe that might possibly have a twisty road. His is a never ending search for twisty roads and breathtaking views.

When he's not riding the Alps, Hermann lives in Coronado, California, a small island off the coast of San Diego. Initially sent there by the U.S. Navy after he graduated from Vanderbilt University in Nashville, Hermann found the ocean, climate, and (most important) the year-round motorcycling more than enough reason to stay.

Hermann is a former director of the BMWMOA and is currently an Ambassador of the Club. His non-motorcycling activities include surfing, appraising real estate, singing with the San Diego Opera Company, and serving on the board of several philanthropic organizations.

Twice he's participated in the riding school at the Nurburgring in Germany. In California, he has been to riding school at the Willow Springs and Laguna Seca tracks. John rides practically every day.